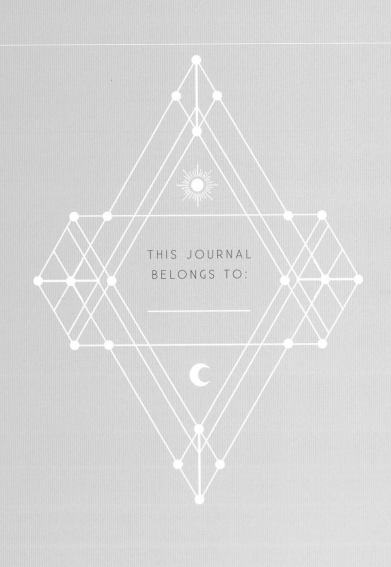

THIS JOURNAL
BELONGS TO:

_____

GRATITUDE

DATE ___/___/___ # EVENING REFLECTION

GOOD THINGS THAT HAPPENED TODAY:

_____

_____

_____

_____

THINGS I DID TO MAKE A POSITIVE DIFFERENCE TODAY:

_____

_____

_____

HOW I FELT TODAY: NOTES:

☐ HAPPY   ☐ NEUTRAL   _____

☐ CONTENT   ☐ INSECURE   _____

☐ PROUD   ☐ DISCOURAGED   _____

☐ HOPEFUL   ☐ DRAINED   _____

☐ LOVING   ☐ SAD   _____

☐ CONNECTED   ☐ SCARED   _____

☐ BALANCED   ☐ ANGRY   _____

☐ JOYFUL   ☐ ANNOYED   _____

☐ RELAXED   ☐ ANXIOUS   _____

☐ CREATIVE   ☐ STRESSED   _____

☐ EXCITED   ☐ OVERWHELMED   _____

☐ _____   ☐ _____

A POSITIVE THOUGHT TO CARRY ME TO SLEEP:

_____

_____

MORNING MEDITATION

DATE ___/___/___

TODAY'S FOCUS:

_____

_____

_____

AN AFFIRMATION FOR TODAY:

_____

_____

_____

WHAT I'M GRATEFUL FOR:

_____

_____

_____

_____

_____

_____

_____

_____

WHAT I'M EXCITED ABOUT TODAY:

_____

_____

_____

HOW I'LL MAKE SPACE FOR GRATITUDE TODAY:

_____

_____

DATE __/__/__ # EVENING REFLECTION

GOOD THINGS THAT HAPPENED TODAY:

_____

_____

_____

_____

THINGS I DID TO MAKE A POSITIVE DIFFERENCE TODAY:

_____

_____

_____

_____

HOW I FELT TODAY: NOTES:

☐ HAPPY   ☐ NEUTRAL   _____

☐ CONTENT   ☐ INSECURE   _____

☐ PROUD   ☐ DISCOURAGED   _____

☐ HOPEFUL   ☐ DRAINED   _____

☐ LOVING   ☐ SAD   _____

☐ CONNECTED   ☐ SCARED   _____

☐ BALANCED   ☐ ANGRY   _____

☐ JOYFUL   ☐ ANNOYED   _____

☐ RELAXED   ☐ ANXIOUS   _____

☐ CREATIVE   ☐ STRESSED   _____

☐ EXCITED   ☐ OVERWHELMED   _____

☐ _____   ☐ _____

A POSITIVE THOUGHT TO CARRY ME TO SLEEP:

_____

_____

MORNING MEDITATION

DATE ___/___/___

TODAY'S FOCUS:

_____

_____

_____

AN AFFIRMATION FOR TODAY:

_____

_____

_____

WHAT I'M GRATEFUL FOR:

_____

_____

_____

_____

_____

_____

_____

_____

WHAT I'M EXCITED ABOUT TODAY:

_____

_____

_____

HOW I'LL MAKE SPACE FOR GRATITUDE TODAY:

_____

_____

DATE __/__/__ # EVENING REFLECTION

GOOD THINGS THAT HAPPENED TODAY:

THINGS I DID TO MAKE A POSITIVE DIFFERENCE TODAY:

HOW I FELT TODAY: NOTES:

- ☐ HAPPY   ☐ NEUTRAL
- ☐ CONTENT   ☐ INSECURE
- ☐ PROUD   ☐ DISCOURAGED
- ☐ HOPEFUL   ☐ DRAINED
- ☐ LOVING   ☐ SAD
- ☐ CONNECTED   ☐ SCARED
- ☐ BALANCED   ☐ ANGRY
- ☐ JOYFUL   ☐ ANNOYED
- ☐ RELAXED   ☐ ANXIOUS
- ☐ CREATIVE   ☐ STRESSED
- ☐ EXCITED   ☐ OVERWHELMED
- ☐ _____   ☐ _____

A POSITIVE THOUGHT TO CARRY ME TO SLEEP:

MORNING MEDITATION

DATE ___/___/___

TODAY'S FOCUS:

_____

_____

_____

_____

AN AFFIRMATION FOR TODAY:

_____

_____

_____

WHAT I'M GRATEFUL FOR:

_____

_____

_____

_____

_____

_____

_____

_____

_____

WHAT I'M EXCITED ABOUT TODAY:

_____

_____

_____

HOW I'LL MAKE SPACE FOR GRATITUDE TODAY:

_____

_____

DATE ___/___/___ # EVENING REFLECTION

GOOD THINGS THAT HAPPENED TODAY:

THINGS I DID TO MAKE A POSITIVE DIFFERENCE TODAY:

HOW I FELT TODAY:

☐ HAPPY		☐ NEUTRAL		
☐ CONTENT		☐ INSECURE		
☐ PROUD		☐ DISCOURAGED		
☐ HOPEFUL		☐ DRAINED		
☐ LOVING		☐ SAD		
☐ CONNECTED		☐ SCARED		
☐ BALANCED		☐ ANGRY		
☐ JOYFUL		☐ ANNOYED		
☐ RELAXED		☐ ANXIOUS		
☐ CREATIVE		☐ STRESSED		
☐ EXCITED		☐ OVERWHELMED		
☐ _____		☐ _____		

NOTES:

A POSITIVE THOUGHT TO CARRY ME TO SLEEP:

MORNING MEDITATION

DATE __/__/__

TODAY'S FOCUS:

AN AFFIRMATION FOR TODAY:

WHAT I'M GRATEFUL FOR:

WHAT I'M EXCITED ABOUT TODAY:

HOW I'LL MAKE SPACE FOR GRATITUDE TODAY:

DATE ___/___/___ # EVENING REFLECTION

GOOD THINGS THAT HAPPENED TODAY:

_____

_____

_____

_____

THINGS I DID TO MAKE A POSITIVE DIFFERENCE TODAY:

_____

_____

_____

_____

HOW I FELT TODAY: NOTES:

☐ HAPPY   ☐ NEUTRAL
☐ CONTENT   ☐ INSECURE
☐ PROUD   ☐ DISCOURAGED
☐ HOPEFUL   ☐ DRAINED
☐ LOVING   ☐ SAD
☐ CONNECTED   ☐ SCARED
☐ BALANCED   ☐ ANGRY
☐ JOYFUL   ☐ ANNOYED
☐ RELAXED   ☐ ANXIOUS
☐ CREATIVE   ☐ STRESSED
☐ EXCITED   ☐ OVERWHELMED
☐ _____   ☐ _____

A POSITIVE THOUGHT TO CARRY ME TO SLEEP:

_____

_____

MORNING MEDITATION

DATE __/__/__

TODAY'S FOCUS:

AN AFFIRMATION FOR TODAY:

WHAT I'M GRATEFUL FOR:

WHAT I'M EXCITED ABOUT TODAY:

HOW I'LL MAKE SPACE FOR GRATITUDE TODAY:

DATE __/__/__   # EVENING REFLECTION

GOOD THINGS THAT HAPPENED TODAY:

_____
_____
_____
_____

THINGS I DID TO MAKE A POSITIVE DIFFERENCE TODAY:

_____
_____
_____

HOW I FELT TODAY: NOTES:

☐ HAPPY	☐ NEUTRAL	_____
☐ CONTENT	☐ INSECURE	_____
☐ PROUD	☐ DISCOURAGED	_____
☐ HOPEFUL	☐ DRAINED	_____
☐ LOVING	☐ SAD	_____
☐ CONNECTED	☐ SCARED	_____
☐ BALANCED	☐ ANGRY	_____
☐ JOYFUL	☐ ANNOYED	_____
☐ RELAXED	☐ ANXIOUS	_____
☐ CREATIVE	☐ STRESSED	_____
☐ EXCITED	☐ OVERWHELMED	_____
☐ _____	☐ _____	

A POSITIVE THOUGHT TO CARRY ME TO SLEEP:

_____
_____
_____

MORNING MEDITATION

DATE ___/___/___

TODAY'S FOCUS:

_____
_____
_____
_____

AN AFFIRMATION FOR TODAY:

_____
_____
_____

WHAT I'M GRATEFUL FOR:

_____
_____
_____
_____
_____
_____
_____
_____
_____

WHAT I'M EXCITED ABOUT TODAY:

_____
_____
_____

HOW I'LL MAKE SPACE FOR GRATITUDE TODAY:

_____
_____

DATE ___/___/___ # EVENING REFLECTION

GOOD THINGS THAT HAPPENED TODAY:

_____

_____

_____

_____

THINGS I DID TO MAKE A POSITIVE DIFFERENCE TODAY:

_____

_____

_____

_____

HOW I FELT TODAY: NOTES:

☐ HAPPY   ☐ NEUTRAL   _____

☐ CONTENT   ☐ INSECURE   _____

☐ PROUD   ☐ DISCOURAGED   _____

☐ HOPEFUL   ☐ DRAINED   _____

☐ LOVING   ☐ SAD   _____

☐ CONNECTED   ☐ SCARED   _____

☐ BALANCED   ☐ ANGRY   _____

☐ JOYFUL   ☐ ANNOYED   _____

☐ RELAXED   ☐ ANXIOUS   _____

☐ CREATIVE   ☐ STRESSED   _____

☐ EXCITED   ☐ OVERWHELMED   _____

☐ _____   ☐ _____   _____

A POSITIVE THOUGHT TO CARRY ME TO SLEEP:

_____

_____

MORNING MEDITATION

DATE ___/___/___

TODAY'S FOCUS:

_____

_____

_____

_____

AN AFFIRMATION FOR TODAY:

_____

_____

_____

WHAT I'M GRATEFUL FOR:

_____

_____

_____

_____

_____

_____

_____

_____

WHAT I'M EXCITED ABOUT TODAY:

_____

_____

_____

HOW I'LL MAKE SPACE FOR GRATITUDE TODAY:

_____

_____

_____

DATE ___/___/___ # EVENING REFLECTION

GOOD THINGS THAT HAPPENED TODAY:
_____
_____
_____
_____

THINGS I DID TO MAKE A POSITIVE DIFFERENCE TODAY:
_____
_____
_____
_____

HOW I FELT TODAY:

NOTES:

- ☐ HAPPY
- ☐ CONTENT
- ☐ PROUD
- ☐ HOPEFUL
- ☐ LOVING
- ☐ CONNECTED
- ☐ BALANCED
- ☐ JOYFUL
- ☐ RELAXED
- ☐ CREATIVE
- ☐ EXCITED
- ☐ _____

- ☐ NEUTRAL
- ☐ INSECURE
- ☐ DISCOURAGED
- ☐ DRAINED
- ☐ SAD
- ☐ SCARED
- ☐ ANGRY
- ☐ ANNOYED
- ☐ ANXIOUS
- ☐ STRESSED
- ☐ OVERWHELMED
- ☐ _____

_____
_____
_____
_____
_____
_____
_____
_____
_____
_____
_____

A POSITIVE THOUGHT TO CARRY ME TO SLEEP:
_____
_____
_____

MORNING MEDITATION

DATE __/__/__

TODAY'S FOCUS:

_____
_____
_____
_____

AN AFFIRMATION FOR TODAY:

_____
_____
_____
_____

WHAT I'M GRATEFUL FOR:

_____
_____
_____
_____
_____
_____
_____
_____

WHAT I'M EXCITED ABOUT TODAY:

_____
_____
_____

HOW I'LL MAKE SPACE FOR GRATITUDE TODAY:

_____
_____

DATE __/__/__ # EVENING REFLECTION

GOOD THINGS THAT HAPPENED TODAY:

THINGS I DID TO MAKE A POSITIVE DIFFERENCE TODAY:

HOW I FELT TODAY:

NOTES:

- ☐ HAPPY
- ☐ CONTENT
- ☐ PROUD
- ☐ HOPEFUL
- ☐ LOVING
- ☐ CONNECTED
- ☐ BALANCED
- ☐ JOYFUL
- ☐ RELAXED
- ☐ CREATIVE
- ☐ EXCITED
- ☐ _____

- ☐ NEUTRAL
- ☐ INSECURE
- ☐ DISCOURAGED
- ☐ DRAINED
- ☐ SAD
- ☐ SCARED
- ☐ ANGRY
- ☐ ANNOYED
- ☐ ANXIOUS
- ☐ STRESSED
- ☐ OVERWHELMED
- ☐ _____

A POSITIVE THOUGHT TO CARRY ME TO SLEEP:

MORNING MEDITATION

DATE __/__/__

TODAY'S FOCUS:

AN AFFIRMATION FOR TODAY:

WHAT I'M GRATEFUL FOR:

WHAT I'M EXCITED ABOUT TODAY:

HOW I'LL MAKE SPACE FOR GRATITUDE TODAY:

DATE __/__/__ # EVENING REFLECTION

GOOD THINGS THAT HAPPENED TODAY:

_____
_____
_____
_____

THINGS I DID TO MAKE A POSITIVE DIFFERENCE TODAY:

_____
_____
_____

HOW I FELT TODAY:

NOTES:

- ☐ HAPPY
- ☐ CONTENT
- ☐ PROUD
- ☐ HOPEFUL
- ☐ LOVING
- ☐ CONNECTED
- ☐ BALANCED
- ☐ JOYFUL
- ☐ RELAXED
- ☐ CREATIVE
- ☐ EXCITED
- ☐ _____

- ☐ NEUTRAL
- ☐ INSECURE
- ☐ DISCOURAGED
- ☐ DRAINED
- ☐ SAD
- ☐ SCARED
- ☐ ANGRY
- ☐ ANNOYED
- ☐ ANXIOUS
- ☐ STRESSED
- ☐ OVERWHELMED
- ☐ _____

_____
_____
_____
_____
_____
_____
_____
_____
_____
_____

A POSITIVE THOUGHT TO CARRY ME TO SLEEP:

_____
_____

MORNING MEDITATION

DATE __/__/__

TODAY'S FOCUS:

_____

_____

_____

AN AFFIRMATION FOR TODAY:

_____

_____

_____

WHAT I'M GRATEFUL FOR:

_____

_____

_____

_____

_____

_____

_____

WHAT I'M EXCITED ABOUT TODAY:

_____

_____

_____

HOW I'LL MAKE SPACE FOR GRATITUDE TODAY:

_____

_____

DATE __/__/__ # EVENING REFLECTION

GOOD THINGS THAT HAPPENED TODAY:
_____
_____
_____
_____

THINGS I DID TO MAKE A POSITIVE DIFFERENCE TODAY:
_____
_____
_____

HOW I FELT TODAY:

NOTES:

- ☐ HAPPY
- ☐ CONTENT
- ☐ PROUD
- ☐ HOPEFUL
- ☐ LOVING
- ☐ CONNECTED
- ☐ BALANCED
- ☐ JOYFUL
- ☐ RELAXED
- ☐ CREATIVE
- ☐ EXCITED
- ☐ _____

- ☐ NEUTRAL
- ☐ INSECURE
- ☐ DISCOURAGED
- ☐ DRAINED
- ☐ SAD
- ☐ SCARED
- ☐ ANGRY
- ☐ ANNOYED
- ☐ ANXIOUS
- ☐ STRESSED
- ☐ OVERWHELMED
- ☐ _____

_____
_____
_____
_____
_____
_____
_____
_____
_____
_____

A POSITIVE THOUGHT TO CARRY ME TO SLEEP:
_____
_____

MORNING MEDITATION

DATE ___/___/___

TODAY'S FOCUS:

_____
_____
_____
_____

AN AFFIRMATION FOR TODAY:

_____
_____
_____
_____

WHAT I'M GRATEFUL FOR:

_____
_____
_____
_____
_____
_____
_____
_____

WHAT I'M EXCITED ABOUT TODAY:

_____
_____
_____

HOW I'LL MAKE SPACE FOR GRATITUDE TODAY:

_____
_____

DATE __/__/__ # EVENING REFLECTION

GOOD THINGS THAT HAPPENED TODAY:

_____

_____

_____

_____

THINGS I DID TO MAKE A POSITIVE DIFFERENCE TODAY:

_____

_____

_____

HOW I FELT TODAY:

NOTES:

- ☐ HAPPY
- ☐ CONTENT
- ☐ PROUD
- ☐ HOPEFUL
- ☐ LOVING
- ☐ CONNECTED
- ☐ BALANCED
- ☐ JOYFUL
- ☐ RELAXED
- ☐ CREATIVE
- ☐ EXCITED
- ☐ _____

- ☐ NEUTRAL
- ☐ INSECURE
- ☐ DISCOURAGED
- ☐ DRAINED
- ☐ SAD
- ☐ SCARED
- ☐ ANGRY
- ☐ ANNOYED
- ☐ ANXIOUS
- ☐ STRESSED
- ☐ OVERWHELMED
- ☐ _____

_____

_____

_____

_____

_____

_____

_____

_____

_____

_____

_____

A POSITIVE THOUGHT TO CARRY ME TO SLEEP:

_____

_____

MORNING MEDITATION

DATE __/__/__

TODAY'S FOCUS:

_____
_____
_____
_____

AN AFFIRMATION FOR TODAY:

_____
_____
_____
_____

WHAT I'M GRATEFUL FOR:

_____
_____
_____
_____
_____
_____
_____
_____
_____

WHAT I'M EXCITED ABOUT TODAY:

_____
_____
_____
_____

HOW I'LL MAKE SPACE FOR GRATITUDE TODAY:

_____
_____

DATE ___/___/___ # EVENING REFLECTION

GOOD THINGS THAT HAPPENED TODAY:

THINGS I DID TO MAKE A POSITIVE DIFFERENCE TODAY:

HOW I FELT TODAY:

☐ HAPPY	☐ NEUTRAL		NOTES:
☐ CONTENT	☐ INSECURE		
☐ PROUD	☐ DISCOURAGED		
☐ HOPEFUL	☐ DRAINED		
☐ LOVING	☐ SAD		
☐ CONNECTED	☐ SCARED		
☐ BALANCED	☐ ANGRY		
☐ JOYFUL	☐ ANNOYED		
☐ RELAXED	☐ ANXIOUS		
☐ CREATIVE	☐ STRESSED		
☐ EXCITED	☐ OVERWHELMED		
☐ _____	☐ _____		

A POSITIVE THOUGHT TO CARRY ME TO SLEEP:

MORNING MEDITATION

DATE ___/___/___

TODAY'S FOCUS:

_____
_____
_____
_____

AN AFFIRMATION FOR TODAY:

_____
_____
_____
_____

WHAT I'M GRATEFUL FOR:

_____
_____
_____
_____
_____
_____
_____
_____

WHAT I'M EXCITED ABOUT TODAY:

_____
_____
_____
_____

HOW I'LL MAKE SPACE FOR GRATITUDE TODAY:

_____
_____
_____

DATE ___/___/___ # EVENING REFLECTION

GOOD THINGS THAT HAPPENED TODAY:
_____
_____
_____
_____

THINGS I DID TO MAKE A POSITIVE DIFFERENCE TODAY:
_____
_____
_____
_____

HOW I FELT TODAY:

NOTES:

- ☐ HAPPY
- ☐ CONTENT
- ☐ PROUD
- ☐ HOPEFUL
- ☐ LOVING
- ☐ CONNECTED
- ☐ BALANCED
- ☐ JOYFUL
- ☐ RELAXED
- ☐ CREATIVE
- ☐ EXCITED
- ☐ _____

- ☐ NEUTRAL
- ☐ INSECURE
- ☐ DISCOURAGED
- ☐ DRAINED
- ☐ SAD
- ☐ SCARED
- ☐ ANGRY
- ☐ ANNOYED
- ☐ ANXIOUS
- ☐ STRESSED
- ☐ OVERWHELMED
- ☐ _____

_____
_____
_____
_____
_____
_____
_____
_____
_____
_____

A POSITIVE THOUGHT TO CARRY ME TO SLEEP:
_____
_____
_____

MORNING MEDITATION

DATE ___/___/___

TODAY'S FOCUS:

_____

_____

_____

_____

AN AFFIRMATION FOR TODAY:

_____

_____

_____

_____

WHAT I'M GRATEFUL FOR:

_____

_____

_____

_____

_____

_____

_____

_____

WHAT I'M EXCITED ABOUT TODAY:

_____

_____

_____

HOW I'LL MAKE SPACE FOR GRATITUDE TODAY:

_____

_____

_____

DATE ___/___/___ # EVENING REFLECTION

GOOD THINGS THAT HAPPENED TODAY:

THINGS I DID TO MAKE A POSITIVE DIFFERENCE TODAY:

HOW I FELT TODAY:

NOTES:

- ☐ HAPPY
- ☐ CONTENT
- ☐ PROUD
- ☐ HOPEFUL
- ☐ LOVING
- ☐ CONNECTED
- ☐ BALANCED
- ☐ JOYFUL
- ☐ RELAXED
- ☐ CREATIVE
- ☐ EXCITED
- ☐ _____

- ☐ NEUTRAL
- ☐ INSECURE
- ☐ DISCOURAGED
- ☐ DRAINED
- ☐ SAD
- ☐ SCARED
- ☐ ANGRY
- ☐ ANNOYED
- ☐ ANXIOUS
- ☐ STRESSED
- ☐ OVERWHELMED
- ☐ _____

A POSITIVE THOUGHT TO CARRY ME TO SLEEP:

MORNING MEDITATION

DATE ___/___/___

TODAY'S FOCUS:

_____

_____

_____

_____

AN AFFIRMATION FOR TODAY:

_____

_____

_____

WHAT I'M GRATEFUL FOR:

_____

_____

_____

_____

_____

_____

_____

WHAT I'M EXCITED ABOUT TODAY:

_____

_____

_____

HOW I'LL MAKE SPACE FOR GRATITUDE TODAY:

_____

_____

DATE ___/___/___ # EVENING REFLECTION

GOOD THINGS THAT HAPPENED TODAY:

_____
_____
_____
_____

THINGS I DID TO MAKE A POSITIVE DIFFERENCE TODAY:

_____
_____
_____

HOW I FELT TODAY:

☐ HAPPY   ☐ NEUTRAL

☐ CONTENT   ☐ INSECURE   **NOTES:**

☐ PROUD   ☐ DISCOURAGED

☐ HOPEFUL   ☐ DRAINED   _____

☐ LOVING   ☐ SAD   _____

☐ CONNECTED   ☐ SCARED   _____

☐ BALANCED   ☐ ANGRY   _____

☐ JOYFUL   ☐ ANNOYED   _____

☐ RELAXED   ☐ ANXIOUS   _____

☐ CREATIVE   ☐ STRESSED   _____

☐ EXCITED   ☐ OVERWHELMED   _____

☐ _____   ☐ _____   _____

A POSITIVE THOUGHT TO CARRY ME TO SLEEP:

_____
_____

MORNING MEDITATION

DATE ___/___/___

TODAY'S FOCUS:

_____
_____
_____
_____

AN AFFIRMATION FOR TODAY:

_____
_____
_____
_____

WHAT I'M GRATEFUL FOR:

_____
_____
_____
_____
_____
_____
_____
_____
_____

WHAT I'M EXCITED ABOUT TODAY:

_____
_____
_____

HOW I'LL MAKE SPACE FOR GRATITUDE TODAY:

_____
_____
_____

DATE __/__/__ # EVENING REFLECTION

GOOD THINGS THAT HAPPENED TODAY:

THINGS I DID TO MAKE A POSITIVE DIFFERENCE TODAY:

HOW I FELT TODAY:

☐ HAPPY	☐ NEUTRAL	
☐ CONTENT	☐ INSECURE	
☐ PROUD	☐ DISCOURAGED	
☐ HOPEFUL	☐ DRAINED	
☐ LOVING	☐ SAD	
☐ CONNECTED	☐ SCARED	
☐ BALANCED	☐ ANGRY	
☐ JOYFUL	☐ ANNOYED	
☐ RELAXED	☐ ANXIOUS	
☐ CREATIVE	☐ STRESSED	
☐ EXCITED	☐ OVERWHELMED	
☐ _____	☐ _____	

A POSITIVE THOUGHT TO CARRY ME TO SLEEP:

MORNING MEDITATION

TODAY'S FOCUS:
_____
_____
_____
_____

AN AFFIRMATION FOR TODAY:
_____
_____
_____
_____

WHAT I'M GRATEFUL FOR:
_____
_____
_____
_____
_____
_____
_____
_____
_____

WHAT I'M EXCITED ABOUT TODAY:
_____
_____
_____

HOW I'LL MAKE SPACE FOR GRATITUDE TODAY:
_____
_____
_____

DATE ___/___/___ # EVENING REFLECTION

GOOD THINGS THAT HAPPENED TODAY:

THINGS I DID TO MAKE A POSITIVE DIFFERENCE TODAY:

HOW I FELT TODAY:

☐ HAPPY	☐ NEUTRAL
☐ CONTENT	☐ INSECURE
☐ PROUD	☐ DISCOURAGED
☐ HOPEFUL	☐ DRAINED
☐ LOVING	☐ SAD
☐ CONNECTED	☐ SCARED
☐ BALANCED	☐ ANGRY
☐ JOYFUL	☐ ANNOYED
☐ RELAXED	☐ ANXIOUS
☐ CREATIVE	☐ STRESSED
☐ EXCITED	☐ OVERWHELMED
☐ _____	☐ _____

A POSITIVE THOUGHT TO CARRY ME TO SLEEP:

MORNING MEDITATION

DATE ___/___/___

TODAY'S FOCUS:

_____

_____

_____

_____

AN AFFIRMATION FOR TODAY:

_____

_____

_____

_____

WHAT I'M GRATEFUL FOR:

_____

_____

_____

_____

_____

_____

_____

_____

WHAT I'M EXCITED ABOUT TODAY:

_____

_____

_____

HOW I'LL MAKE SPACE FOR GRATITUDE TODAY:

_____

_____

DATE __/__/__   # EVENING REFLECTION

GOOD THINGS THAT HAPPENED TODAY:

THINGS I DID TO MAKE A POSITIVE DIFFERENCE TODAY:

HOW I FELT TODAY:

☐ HAPPY	☐ NEUTRAL
☐ CONTENT	☐ INSECURE
☐ PROUD	☐ DISCOURAGED
☐ HOPEFUL	☐ DRAINED
☐ LOVING	☐ SAD
☐ CONNECTED	☐ SCARED
☐ BALANCED	☐ ANGRY
☐ JOYFUL	☐ ANNOYED
☐ RELAXED	☐ ANXIOUS
☐ CREATIVE	☐ STRESSED
☐ EXCITED	☐ OVERWHELMED
☐ _____	☐ _____

A POSITIVE THOUGHT TO CARRY ME TO SLEEP:

MORNING MEDITATION

DATE ___/___/___

TODAY'S FOCUS:

_____
_____
_____
_____

AN AFFIRMATION FOR TODAY:

_____
_____
_____
_____

WHAT I'M GRATEFUL FOR:

_____
_____
_____
_____
_____
_____
_____
_____

WHAT I'M EXCITED ABOUT TODAY:

_____
_____
_____

HOW I'LL MAKE SPACE FOR GRATITUDE TODAY:

_____
_____

DATE ___/___/___ # EVENING REFLECTION

GOOD THINGS THAT HAPPENED TODAY:

THINGS I DID TO MAKE A POSITIVE DIFFERENCE TODAY:

HOW I FELT TODAY:

☐ HAPPY	☐ NEUTRAL
☐ CONTENT	☐ INSECURE
☐ PROUD	☐ DISCOURAGED
☐ HOPEFUL	☐ DRAINED
☐ LOVING	☐ SAD
☐ CONNECTED	☐ SCARED
☐ BALANCED	☐ ANGRY
☐ JOYFUL	☐ ANNOYED
☐ RELAXED	☐ ANXIOUS
☐ CREATIVE	☐ STRESSED
☐ EXCITED	☐ OVERWHELMED
☐ _____	☐ _____

A POSITIVE THOUGHT TO CARRY ME TO SLEEP:

MORNING MEDITATION

DATE __/__/__

TODAY'S FOCUS:

AN AFFIRMATION FOR TODAY:

WHAT I'M GRATEFUL FOR:

WHAT I'M EXCITED ABOUT TODAY:

HOW I'LL MAKE SPACE FOR GRATITUDE TODAY:

DATE __/__/__ # EVENING REFLECTION

GOOD THINGS THAT HAPPENED TODAY:

_____

_____

_____

THINGS I DID TO MAKE A POSITIVE DIFFERENCE TODAY:

_____

_____

_____

HOW I FELT TODAY:

- ☐ HAPPY
- ☐ CONTENT
- ☐ PROUD
- ☐ HOPEFUL
- ☐ LOVING
- ☐ CONNECTED
- ☐ BALANCED
- ☐ JOYFUL
- ☐ RELAXED
- ☐ CREATIVE
- ☐ EXCITED
- ☐ _____

- ☐ NEUTRAL
- ☐ INSECURE
- ☐ DISCOURAGED
- ☐ DRAINED
- ☐ SAD
- ☐ SCARED
- ☐ ANGRY
- ☐ ANNOYED
- ☐ ANXIOUS
- ☐ STRESSED
- ☐ OVERWHELMED
- ☐ _____

A POSITIVE THOUGHT TO CARRY ME TO SLEEP:

_____

_____

MORNING MEDITATION

DATE ___/___/___

TODAY'S FOCUS:

_____
_____
_____
_____

AN AFFIRMATION FOR TODAY:

_____
_____
_____
_____

WHAT I'M GRATEFUL FOR:

_____
_____
_____
_____
_____
_____
_____
_____
_____
_____

WHAT I'M EXCITED ABOUT TODAY:

_____
_____
_____

HOW I'LL MAKE SPACE FOR GRATITUDE TODAY:

_____
_____

DATE ___/___/___ # EVENING REFLECTION

GOOD THINGS THAT HAPPENED TODAY:

_____
_____
_____
_____

THINGS I DID TO MAKE A POSITIVE DIFFERENCE TODAY:

_____
_____
_____
_____

HOW I FELT TODAY:

☐ HAPPY ☐ NEUTRAL

☐ CONTENT ☐ INSECURE

☐ PROUD ☐ DISCOURAGED

☐ HOPEFUL ☐ DRAINED

☐ LOVING ☐ SAD

☐ CONNECTED ☐ SCARED

☐ BALANCED ☐ ANGRY

☐ JOYFUL ☐ ANNOYED

☐ RELAXED ☐ ANXIOUS

☐ CREATIVE ☐ STRESSED

☐ EXCITED ☐ OVERWHELMED

☐ _____ ☐ _____

A POSITIVE THOUGHT TO CARRY ME TO SLEEP:

_____
_____
_____

MORNING MEDITATION

DATE ___/___/___

TODAY'S FOCUS:

_____
_____
_____
_____

AN AFFIRMATION FOR TODAY:

_____
_____
_____
_____

WHAT I'M GRATEFUL FOR:

_____
_____
_____
_____
_____
_____
_____
_____

WHAT I'M EXCITED ABOUT TODAY:

_____
_____
_____

HOW I'LL MAKE SPACE FOR GRATITUDE TODAY:

_____
_____

DATE __/__/__ # EVENING REFLECTION

GOOD THINGS THAT HAPPENED TODAY:

THINGS I DID TO MAKE A POSITIVE DIFFERENCE TODAY:

HOW I FELT TODAY:

☐ HAPPY	☐ NEUTRAL
☐ CONTENT	☐ INSECURE
☐ PROUD	☐ DISCOURAGED
☐ HOPEFUL	☐ DRAINED
☐ LOVING	☐ SAD
☐ CONNECTED	☐ SCARED
☐ BALANCED	☐ ANGRY
☐ JOYFUL	☐ ANNOYED
☐ RELAXED	☐ ANXIOUS
☐ CREATIVE	☐ STRESSED
☐ EXCITED	☐ OVERWHELMED
☐ _____	☐ _____

A POSITIVE THOUGHT TO CARRY ME TO SLEEP:

MORNING MEDITATION

DATE ___/___/___

TODAY'S FOCUS:

_____

_____

_____

_____

AN AFFIRMATION FOR TODAY:

_____

_____

_____

_____

WHAT I'M GRATEFUL FOR:

_____

_____

_____

_____

_____

_____

_____

_____

WHAT I'M EXCITED ABOUT TODAY:

_____

_____

_____

_____

HOW I'LL MAKE SPACE FOR GRATITUDE TODAY:

_____

_____

_____

DATE ___/___/___   EVENING REFLECTION

GOOD THINGS THAT HAPPENED TODAY:

THINGS I DID TO MAKE A POSITIVE DIFFERENCE TODAY:

HOW I FELT TODAY:

☐ HAPPY   ☐ NEUTRAL
☐ CONTENT   ☐ INSECURE
☐ PROUD   ☐ DISCOURAGED
☐ HOPEFUL   ☐ DRAINED
☐ LOVING   ☐ SAD
☐ CONNECTED   ☐ SCARED
☐ BALANCED   ☐ ANGRY
☐ JOYFUL   ☐ ANNOYED
☐ RELAXED   ☐ ANXIOUS
☐ CREATIVE   ☐ STRESSED
☐ EXCITED   ☐ OVERWHELMED
☐ _____   ☐ _____

A POSITIVE THOUGHT TO CARRY ME TO SLEEP:

MORNING MEDITATION

DATE ___/___/___

TODAY'S FOCUS:

_____

_____

_____

_____

AN AFFIRMATION FOR TODAY:

_____

_____

_____

_____

WHAT I'M GRATEFUL FOR:

_____

_____

_____

_____

_____

_____

_____

_____

_____

WHAT I'M EXCITED ABOUT TODAY:

_____

_____

_____

HOW I'LL MAKE SPACE FOR GRATITUDE TODAY:

_____

_____

DATE ___/___/___ # EVENING REFLECTION

GOOD THINGS THAT HAPPENED TODAY:

THINGS I DID TO MAKE A POSITIVE DIFFERENCE TODAY:

HOW I FELT TODAY:

- ☐ HAPPY
- ☐ CONTENT
- ☐ PROUD
- ☐ HOPEFUL
- ☐ LOVING
- ☐ CONNECTED
- ☐ BALANCED
- ☐ JOYFUL
- ☐ RELAXED
- ☐ CREATIVE
- ☐ EXCITED
- ☐ _____

- ☐ NEUTRAL
- ☐ INSECURE
- ☐ DISCOURAGED
- ☐ DRAINED
- ☐ SAD
- ☐ SCARED
- ☐ ANGRY
- ☐ ANNOYED
- ☐ ANXIOUS
- ☐ STRESSED
- ☐ OVERWHELMED
- ☐ _____

A POSITIVE THOUGHT TO CARRY ME TO SLEEP:

MORNING MEDITATION

DATE ___/___/___

TODAY'S FOCUS:
_____
_____
_____
_____

AN AFFIRMATION FOR TODAY:
_____
_____
_____
_____

WHAT I'M GRATEFUL FOR:
_____
_____
_____
_____
_____
_____
_____
_____

WHAT I'M EXCITED ABOUT TODAY:
_____
_____
_____

HOW I'LL MAKE SPACE FOR GRATITUDE TODAY:
_____
_____

DATE ___/___/___ # EVENING REFLECTION

GOOD THINGS THAT HAPPENED TODAY:

THINGS I DID TO MAKE A POSITIVE DIFFERENCE TODAY:

HOW I FELT TODAY:

☐ HAPPY	☐ NEUTRAL
☐ CONTENT	☐ INSECURE
☐ PROUD	☐ DISCOURAGED
☐ HOPEFUL	☐ DRAINED
☐ LOVING	☐ SAD
☐ CONNECTED	☐ SCARED
☐ BALANCED	☐ ANGRY
☐ JOYFUL	☐ ANNOYED
☐ RELAXED	☐ ANXIOUS
☐ CREATIVE	☐ STRESSED
☐ EXCITED	☐ OVERWHELMED
☐ _____	☐ _____

A POSITIVE THOUGHT TO CARRY ME TO SLEEP:

MORNING MEDITATION

DATE ___/___/___

TODAY'S FOCUS:

_____
_____
_____
_____

AN AFFIRMATION FOR TODAY:

_____
_____
_____
_____

WHAT I'M GRATEFUL FOR:

_____
_____
_____
_____
_____
_____
_____
_____

WHAT I'M EXCITED ABOUT TODAY:

_____
_____
_____

HOW I'LL MAKE SPACE FOR GRATITUDE TODAY:

_____
_____

DATE __/__/__ # EVENING REFLECTION

GOOD THINGS THAT HAPPENED TODAY:

THINGS I DID TO MAKE A POSITIVE DIFFERENCE TODAY:

HOW I FELT TODAY:

☐ HAPPY
☐ CONTENT
☐ PROUD
☐ HOPEFUL
☐ LOVING
☐ CONNECTED
☐ BALANCED
☐ JOYFUL
☐ RELAXED
☐ CREATIVE
☐ EXCITED
☐ _____

☐ NEUTRAL
☐ INSECURE
☐ DISCOURAGED
☐ DRAINED
☐ SAD
☐ SCARED
☐ ANGRY
☐ ANNOYED
☐ ANXIOUS
☐ STRESSED
☐ OVERWHELMED
☐ _____

A POSITIVE THOUGHT TO CARRY ME TO SLEEP:

MORNING MEDITATION

DATE ___/___/___

TODAY'S FOCUS:

_____
_____
_____
_____

AN AFFIRMATION FOR TODAY:

_____
_____
_____
_____

WHAT I'M GRATEFUL FOR:

_____
_____
_____
_____
_____
_____
_____
_____

WHAT I'M EXCITED ABOUT TODAY:

_____
_____
_____

HOW I'LL MAKE SPACE FOR GRATITUDE TODAY:

_____
_____

DATE ___/___/___ # EVENING REFLECTION

GOOD THINGS THAT HAPPENED TODAY:

THINGS I DID TO MAKE A POSITIVE DIFFERENCE TODAY:

HOW I FELT TODAY:

☐ HAPPY	☐ NEUTRAL
☐ CONTENT	☐ INSECURE
☐ PROUD	☐ DISCOURAGED
☐ HOPEFUL	☐ DRAINED
☐ LOVING	☐ SAD
☐ CONNECTED	☐ SCARED
☐ BALANCED	☐ ANGRY
☐ JOYFUL	☐ ANNOYED
☐ RELAXED	☐ ANXIOUS
☐ CREATIVE	☐ STRESSED
☐ EXCITED	☐ OVERWHELMED
☐ _____	☐ _____

A POSITIVE THOUGHT TO CARRY ME TO SLEEP:

MORNING MEDITATION

TODAY'S FOCUS:

_____

_____

_____

_____

AN AFFIRMATION FOR TODAY:

_____

_____

_____

_____

WHAT I'M GRATEFUL FOR:

_____

_____

_____

_____

_____

_____

_____

_____

WHAT I'M EXCITED ABOUT TODAY:

_____

_____

_____

HOW I'LL MAKE SPACE FOR GRATITUDE TODAY:

_____

_____

DATE ___/___/___   # EVENING REFLECTION

GOOD THINGS THAT HAPPENED TODAY:

THINGS I DID TO MAKE A POSITIVE DIFFERENCE TODAY:

HOW I FELT TODAY:

☐ HAPPY   ☐ NEUTRAL
☐ CONTENT   ☐ INSECURE
☐ PROUD   ☐ DISCOURAGED
☐ HOPEFUL   ☐ DRAINED
☐ LOVING   ☐ SAD
☐ CONNECTED   ☐ SCARED
☐ BALANCED   ☐ ANGRY
☐ JOYFUL   ☐ ANNOYED
☐ RELAXED   ☐ ANXIOUS
☐ CREATIVE   ☐ STRESSED
☐ EXCITED   ☐ OVERWHELMED
☐ _____   ☐ _____

A POSITIVE THOUGHT TO CARRY ME TO SLEEP:

MORNING MEDITATION

DATE ___/___/___

TODAY'S FOCUS:

AN AFFIRMATION FOR TODAY:

WHAT I'M GRATEFUL FOR:

WHAT I'M EXCITED ABOUT TODAY:

HOW I'LL MAKE SPACE FOR GRATITUDE TODAY:

DATE ___/___/___ # EVENING REFLECTION

GOOD THINGS THAT HAPPENED TODAY:

THINGS I DID TO MAKE A POSITIVE DIFFERENCE TODAY:

HOW I FELT TODAY:

- ☐ HAPPY
- ☐ CONTENT
- ☐ PROUD
- ☐ HOPEFUL
- ☐ LOVING
- ☐ CONNECTED
- ☐ BALANCED
- ☐ JOYFUL
- ☐ RELAXED
- ☐ CREATIVE
- ☐ EXCITED
- ☐ _____

- ☐ NEUTRAL
- ☐ INSECURE
- ☐ DISCOURAGED
- ☐ DRAINED
- ☐ SAD
- ☐ SCARED
- ☐ ANGRY
- ☐ ANNOYED
- ☐ ANXIOUS
- ☐ STRESSED
- ☐ OVERWHELMED
- ☐ _____

A POSITIVE THOUGHT TO CARRY ME TO SLEEP:

MORNING MEDITATION DATE __/__/__

TODAY'S FOCUS:

AN AFFIRMATION FOR TODAY:

WHAT I'M GRATEFUL FOR:

WHAT I'M EXCITED ABOUT TODAY:

HOW I'LL MAKE SPACE FOR GRATITUDE TODAY:

DATE ___/___/___ EVENING REFLECTION

GOOD THINGS THAT HAPPENED TODAY:

_____
_____
_____
_____

THINGS I DID TO MAKE A POSITIVE DIFFERENCE TODAY:

_____
_____
_____

HOW I FELT TODAY:

☐ HAPPY   ☐ NEUTRAL
☐ CONTENT   ☐ INSECURE
☐ PROUD   ☐ DISCOURAGED
☐ HOPEFUL   ☐ DRAINED
☐ LOVING   ☐ SAD
☐ CONNECTED   ☐ SCARED
☐ BALANCED   ☐ ANGRY
☐ JOYFUL   ☐ ANNOYED
☐ RELAXED   ☐ ANXIOUS
☐ CREATIVE   ☐ STRESSED
☐ EXCITED   ☐ OVERWHELMED
☐ _____   ☐ _____

A POSITIVE THOUGHT TO CARRY ME TO SLEEP:

_____
_____

MORNING MEDITATION

TODAY'S FOCUS:

_____
_____
_____
_____

AN AFFIRMATION FOR TODAY:

_____
_____
_____

WHAT I'M GRATEFUL FOR:

_____
_____
_____
_____
_____
_____
_____
_____

WHAT I'M EXCITED ABOUT TODAY:

_____
_____
_____

HOW I'LL MAKE SPACE FOR GRATITUDE TODAY:

_____
_____

EVENING REFLECTION

GOOD THINGS THAT HAPPENED TODAY:

THINGS I DID TO MAKE A POSITIVE DIFFERENCE TODAY:

HOW I FELT TODAY:

- ☐ HAPPY
- ☐ CONTENT
- ☐ PROUD
- ☐ HOPEFUL
- ☐ LOVING
- ☐ CONNECTED
- ☐ BALANCED
- ☐ JOYFUL
- ☐ RELAXED
- ☐ CREATIVE
- ☐ EXCITED
- ☐ _____

- ☐ NEUTRAL
- ☐ INSECURE
- ☐ DISCOURAGED
- ☐ DRAINED
- ☐ SAD
- ☐ SCARED
- ☐ ANGRY
- ☐ ANNOYED
- ☐ ANXIOUS
- ☐ STRESSED
- ☐ OVERWHELMED
- ☐ _____

A POSITIVE THOUGHT TO CARRY ME TO SLEEP:

MORNING MEDITATION

TODAY'S FOCUS:

_____
_____
_____
_____

AN AFFIRMATION FOR TODAY:

_____
_____
_____
_____

WHAT I'M GRATEFUL FOR:

_____
_____
_____
_____
_____
_____
_____
_____

WHAT I'M EXCITED ABOUT TODAY:

_____
_____
_____

HOW I'LL MAKE SPACE FOR GRATITUDE TODAY:

_____
_____
_____

EVENING REFLECTION

GOOD THINGS THAT HAPPENED TODAY:

THINGS I DID TO MAKE A POSITIVE DIFFERENCE TODAY:

HOW I FELT TODAY:

- ☐ HAPPY
- ☐ CONTENT
- ☐ PROUD
- ☐ HOPEFUL
- ☐ LOVING
- ☐ CONNECTED
- ☐ BALANCED
- ☐ JOYFUL
- ☐ RELAXED
- ☐ CREATIVE
- ☐ EXCITED
- ☐ _____

- ☐ NEUTRAL
- ☐ INSECURE
- ☐ DISCOURAGED
- ☐ DRAINED
- ☐ SAD
- ☐ SCARED
- ☐ ANGRY
- ☐ ANNOYED
- ☐ ANXIOUS
- ☐ STRESSED
- ☐ OVERWHELMED
- ☐ _____

A POSITIVE THOUGHT TO CARRY ME TO SLEEP:

MORNING MEDITATION

DATE __/__/__

TODAY'S FOCUS:

AN AFFIRMATION FOR TODAY:

WHAT I'M GRATEFUL FOR:

WHAT I'M EXCITED ABOUT TODAY:

HOW I'LL MAKE SPACE FOR GRATITUDE TODAY:

DATE __/__/__ # EVENING REFLECTION

GOOD THINGS THAT HAPPENED TODAY:

_____

_____

_____

_____

THINGS I DID TO MAKE A POSITIVE DIFFERENCE TODAY:

_____

_____

_____

HOW I FELT TODAY:

- ☐ HAPPY
- ☐ CONTENT
- ☐ PROUD
- ☐ HOPEFUL
- ☐ LOVING
- ☐ CONNECTED
- ☐ BALANCED
- ☐ JOYFUL
- ☐ RELAXED
- ☐ CREATIVE
- ☐ EXCITED
- ☐ _____

- ☐ NEUTRAL
- ☐ INSECURE
- ☐ DISCOURAGED
- ☐ DRAINED
- ☐ SAD
- ☐ SCARED
- ☐ ANGRY
- ☐ ANNOYED
- ☐ ANXIOUS
- ☐ STRESSED
- ☐ OVERWHELMED
- ☐ _____

A POSITIVE THOUGHT TO CARRY ME TO SLEEP:

_____

_____

MORNING MEDITATION

DATE ___/___/___

TODAY'S FOCUS:

_____

_____

_____

_____

AN AFFIRMATION FOR TODAY:

_____

_____

_____

WHAT I'M GRATEFUL FOR:

_____

_____

_____

_____

_____

_____

_____

_____

WHAT I'M EXCITED ABOUT TODAY:

_____

_____

_____

HOW I'LL MAKE SPACE FOR GRATITUDE TODAY:

_____

_____

_____

DATE __/__/__ # EVENING REFLECTION

GOOD THINGS THAT HAPPENED TODAY:
_____
_____
_____
_____

THINGS I DID TO MAKE A POSITIVE DIFFERENCE TODAY:
_____
_____
_____
_____

HOW I FELT TODAY:

NOTES:

☐ HAPPY   ☐ NEUTRAL
☐ CONTENT   ☐ INSECURE   _____
☐ PROUD   ☐ DISCOURAGED   _____
☐ HOPEFUL   ☐ DRAINED   _____
☐ LOVING   ☐ SAD   _____
☐ CONNECTED   ☐ SCARED   _____
☐ BALANCED   ☐ ANGRY   _____
☐ JOYFUL   ☐ ANNOYED   _____
☐ RELAXED   ☐ ANXIOUS   _____
☐ CREATIVE   ☐ STRESSED   _____
☐ EXCITED   ☐ OVERWHELMED   _____
☐ _____   ☐ _____

A POSITIVE THOUGHT TO CARRY ME TO SLEEP:
_____
_____
_____

MORNING MEDITATION
DATE ___/___/___

TODAY'S FOCUS:

_____

_____

_____

_____

AN AFFIRMATION FOR TODAY:

_____

_____

_____

_____

WHAT I'M GRATEFUL FOR:

_____

_____

_____

_____

_____

_____

_____

_____

_____

WHAT I'M EXCITED ABOUT TODAY:

_____

_____

_____

_____

HOW I'LL MAKE SPACE FOR GRATITUDE TODAY:

_____

_____

_____

DATE __/__/__ # EVENING REFLECTION

GOOD THINGS THAT HAPPENED TODAY:
_____
_____
_____
_____

THINGS I DID TO MAKE A POSITIVE DIFFERENCE TODAY:
_____
_____
_____
_____

HOW I FELT TODAY:

NOTES:

- ☐ HAPPY
- ☐ CONTENT
- ☐ PROUD
- ☐ HOPEFUL
- ☐ LOVING
- ☐ CONNECTED
- ☐ BALANCED
- ☐ JOYFUL
- ☐ RELAXED
- ☐ CREATIVE
- ☐ EXCITED
- ☐ _____

- ☐ NEUTRAL
- ☐ INSECURE
- ☐ DISCOURAGED
- ☐ DRAINED
- ☐ SAD
- ☐ SCARED
- ☐ ANGRY
- ☐ ANNOYED
- ☐ ANXIOUS
- ☐ STRESSED
- ☐ OVERWHELMED
- ☐ _____

_____
_____
_____
_____
_____
_____
_____
_____
_____
_____

A POSITIVE THOUGHT TO CARRY ME TO SLEEP:
_____
_____
_____

MORNING MEDITATION
DATE ___/___/___

TODAY'S FOCUS:
_____
_____
_____
_____

AN AFFIRMATION FOR TODAY:
_____
_____
_____
_____

WHAT I'M GRATEFUL FOR:
_____
_____
_____
_____
_____
_____
_____
_____

WHAT I'M EXCITED ABOUT TODAY:
_____
_____
_____
_____

HOW I'LL MAKE SPACE FOR GRATITUDE TODAY:
_____
_____
_____

DATE __/__/__ # EVENING REFLECTION

GOOD THINGS THAT HAPPENED TODAY:

THINGS I DID TO MAKE A POSITIVE DIFFERENCE TODAY:

HOW I FELT TODAY:

NOTES:

- ☐ HAPPY
- ☐ CONTENT
- ☐ PROUD
- ☐ HOPEFUL
- ☐ LOVING
- ☐ CONNECTED
- ☐ BALANCED
- ☐ JOYFUL
- ☐ RELAXED
- ☐ CREATIVE
- ☐ EXCITED
- ☐ _____

- ☐ NEUTRAL
- ☐ INSECURE
- ☐ DISCOURAGED
- ☐ DRAINED
- ☐ SAD
- ☐ SCARED
- ☐ ANGRY
- ☐ ANNOYED
- ☐ ANXIOUS
- ☐ STRESSED
- ☐ OVERWHELMED
- ☐ _____

A POSITIVE THOUGHT TO CARRY ME TO SLEEP:

MORNING MEDITATION

DATE ___/___/___

TODAY'S FOCUS:

AN AFFIRMATION FOR TODAY:

WHAT I'M GRATEFUL FOR:

WHAT I'M EXCITED ABOUT TODAY:

HOW I'LL MAKE SPACE FOR GRATITUDE TODAY:

DATE __/__/__ # EVENING REFLECTION

GOOD THINGS THAT HAPPENED TODAY:

_____

_____

_____

_____

THINGS I DID TO MAKE A POSITIVE DIFFERENCE TODAY:

_____

_____

_____

_____

HOW I FELT TODAY:

NOTES:

☐ HAPPY   ☐ NEUTRAL
☐ CONTENT   ☐ INSECURE   _____
☐ PROUD   ☐ DISCOURAGED   _____
☐ HOPEFUL   ☐ DRAINED   _____
☐ LOVING   ☐ SAD   _____
☐ CONNECTED   ☐ SCARED   _____
☐ BALANCED   ☐ ANGRY   _____
☐ JOYFUL   ☐ ANNOYED   _____
☐ RELAXED   ☐ ANXIOUS   _____
☐ CREATIVE   ☐ STRESSED   _____
☐ EXCITED   ☐ OVERWHELMED   _____
☐ _____   ☐ _____

A POSITIVE THOUGHT TO CARRY ME TO SLEEP:

_____

_____

_____

MORNING MEDITATION

TODAY'S FOCUS:

_____

_____

_____

_____

AN AFFIRMATION FOR TODAY:

_____

_____

_____

_____

WHAT I'M GRATEFUL FOR:

_____

_____

_____

_____

_____

_____

_____

_____

WHAT I'M EXCITED ABOUT TODAY:

_____

_____

_____

HOW I'LL MAKE SPACE FOR GRATITUDE TODAY:

_____

_____

_____

EVENING REFLECTION

GOOD THINGS THAT HAPPENED TODAY:

THINGS I DID TO MAKE A POSITIVE DIFFERENCE TODAY:

HOW I FELT TODAY:

☐ HAPPY	☐ NEUTRAL
☐ CONTENT	☐ INSECURE
☐ PROUD	☐ DISCOURAGED
☐ HOPEFUL	☐ DRAINED
☐ LOVING	☐ SAD
☐ CONNECTED	☐ SCARED
☐ BALANCED	☐ ANGRY
☐ JOYFUL	☐ ANNOYED
☐ RELAXED	☐ ANXIOUS
☐ CREATIVE	☐ STRESSED
☐ EXCITED	☐ OVERWHELMED
☐ _____	☐ _____

NOTES:

A POSITIVE THOUGHT TO CARRY ME TO SLEEP:

MORNING MEDITATION

DATE __ / __ / __

TODAY'S FOCUS:

AN AFFIRMATION FOR TODAY:

WHAT I'M GRATEFUL FOR:

WHAT I'M EXCITED ABOUT TODAY:

HOW I'LL MAKE SPACE FOR GRATITUDE TODAY:

DATE __/__/__ # EVENING REFLECTION

GOOD THINGS THAT HAPPENED TODAY:

_____

_____

_____

_____

THINGS I DID TO MAKE A POSITIVE DIFFERENCE TODAY:

_____

_____

_____

_____

HOW I FELT TODAY:

☐ HAPPY   ☐ NEUTRAL   NOTES:
☐ CONTENT   ☐ INSECURE
☐ PROUD   ☐ DISCOURAGED   _____
☐ HOPEFUL   ☐ DRAINED   _____
☐ LOVING   ☐ SAD   _____
☐ CONNECTED   ☐ SCARED   _____
☐ BALANCED   ☐ ANGRY   _____
☐ JOYFUL   ☐ ANNOYED   _____
☐ RELAXED   ☐ ANXIOUS   _____
☐ CREATIVE   ☐ STRESSED   _____
☐ EXCITED   ☐ OVERWHELMED   _____
☐ _____   ☐ _____   _____

A POSITIVE THOUGHT TO CARRY ME TO SLEEP:

_____

_____

_____

MORNING MEDITATION   DATE __/__/__

TODAY'S FOCUS:

AN AFFIRMATION FOR TODAY:

WHAT I'M GRATEFUL FOR:

WHAT I'M EXCITED ABOUT TODAY:

HOW I'LL MAKE SPACE FOR GRATITUDE TODAY:

DATE ___/___/___ # EVENING REFLECTION

GOOD THINGS THAT HAPPENED TODAY:

THINGS I DID TO MAKE A POSITIVE DIFFERENCE TODAY:

HOW I FELT TODAY:

☐ HAPPY	☐ NEUTRAL
☐ CONTENT	☐ INSECURE
☐ PROUD	☐ DISCOURAGED
☐ HOPEFUL	☐ DRAINED
☐ LOVING	☐ SAD
☐ CONNECTED	☐ SCARED
☐ BALANCED	☐ ANGRY
☐ JOYFUL	☐ ANNOYED
☐ RELAXED	☐ ANXIOUS
☐ CREATIVE	☐ STRESSED
☐ EXCITED	☐ OVERWHELMED
☐ _____	☐ _____

NOTES:

A POSITIVE THOUGHT TO CARRY ME TO SLEEP:

MORNING MEDITATION DATE __/__/__

TODAY'S FOCUS:

AN AFFIRMATION FOR TODAY:

WHAT I'M GRATEFUL FOR:

WHAT I'M EXCITED ABOUT TODAY:

HOW I'LL MAKE SPACE FOR GRATITUDE TODAY:

DATE ___/___/___　EVENING REFLECTION

GOOD THINGS THAT HAPPENED TODAY:
_____
_____
_____
_____

THINGS I DID TO MAKE A POSITIVE DIFFERENCE TODAY:
_____
_____
_____
_____

HOW I FELT TODAY:

☐ HAPPY　　　　☐ NEUTRAL
☐ CONTENT　　　☐ INSECURE
☐ PROUD　　　　☐ DISCOURAGED
☐ HOPEFUL　　　☐ DRAINED
☐ LOVING　　　　☐ SAD
☐ CONNECTED　　☐ SCARED
☐ BALANCED　　☐ ANGRY
☐ JOYFUL　　　☐ ANNOYED
☐ RELAXED　　☐ ANXIOUS
☐ CREATIVE　　☐ STRESSED
☐ EXCITED　　　☐ OVERWHELMED
☐ _____　☐ _____

NOTES:
_____
_____
_____
_____
_____
_____
_____
_____

A POSITIVE THOUGHT TO CARRY ME TO SLEEP:
_____
_____
_____

MORNING MEDITATION

DATE __/__/__

TODAY'S FOCUS:

_____
_____
_____
_____

AN AFFIRMATION FOR TODAY:

_____
_____
_____

WHAT I'M GRATEFUL FOR:

_____
_____
_____
_____
_____
_____
_____

WHAT I'M EXCITED ABOUT TODAY:

_____
_____
_____

HOW I'LL MAKE SPACE FOR GRATITUDE TODAY:

_____
_____

DATE __/__/__ # EVENING REFLECTION

GOOD THINGS THAT HAPPENED TODAY:

_____

_____

_____

_____

THINGS I DID TO MAKE A POSITIVE DIFFERENCE TODAY:

_____

_____

_____

HOW I FELT TODAY:

NOTES:

☐ HAPPY   ☐ NEUTRAL

☐ CONTENT   ☐ INSECURE   _____

☐ PROUD   ☐ DISCOURAGED   _____

☐ HOPEFUL   ☐ DRAINED   _____

☐ LOVING   ☐ SAD   _____

☐ CONNECTED   ☐ SCARED   _____

☐ BALANCED   ☐ ANGRY   _____

☐ JOYFUL   ☐ ANNOYED   _____

☐ RELAXED   ☐ ANXIOUS   _____

☐ CREATIVE   ☐ STRESSED   _____

☐ EXCITED   ☐ OVERWHELMED   _____

☐ _____   ☐ _____   _____

A POSITIVE THOUGHT TO CARRY ME TO SLEEP:

_____

_____

_____

MORNING MEDITATION

DATE ___/___/___

TODAY'S FOCUS:

_____
_____
_____
_____

AN AFFIRMATION FOR TODAY:

_____
_____
_____
_____

WHAT I'M GRATEFUL FOR:

_____
_____
_____
_____
_____
_____
_____
_____

WHAT I'M EXCITED ABOUT TODAY:

_____
_____
_____

HOW I'LL MAKE SPACE FOR GRATITUDE TODAY:

_____
_____

DATE ___/___/___ # EVENING REFLECTION

GOOD THINGS THAT HAPPENED TODAY:

_____

_____

_____

_____

THINGS I DID TO MAKE A POSITIVE DIFFERENCE TODAY:

_____

_____

_____

HOW I FELT TODAY:

☐ HAPPY	☐ NEUTRAL
☐ CONTENT	☐ INSECURE
☐ PROUD	☐ DISCOURAGED
☐ HOPEFUL	☐ DRAINED
☐ LOVING	☐ SAD
☐ CONNECTED	☐ SCARED
☐ BALANCED	☐ ANGRY
☐ JOYFUL	☐ ANNOYED
☐ RELAXED	☐ ANXIOUS
☐ CREATIVE	☐ STRESSED
☐ EXCITED	☐ OVERWHELMED
☐ _____	☐ _____

A POSITIVE THOUGHT TO CARRY ME TO SLEEP:

_____

_____

_____

MORNING MEDITATION

DATE ___/___/___

TODAY'S FOCUS:

_____
_____
_____

AN AFFIRMATION FOR TODAY:

_____
_____
_____

WHAT I'M GRATEFUL FOR:

_____
_____
_____
_____
_____
_____
_____

WHAT I'M EXCITED ABOUT TODAY:

_____
_____
_____

HOW I'LL MAKE SPACE FOR GRATITUDE TODAY:

_____
_____

DATE ___/___/___ # EVENING REFLECTION

GOOD THINGS THAT HAPPENED TODAY:

_____

_____

_____

_____

THINGS I DID TO MAKE A POSITIVE DIFFERENCE TODAY:

_____

_____

_____

HOW I FELT TODAY:

☐ HAPPY   ☐ NEUTRAL
☐ CONTENT   ☐ INSECURE
☐ PROUD   ☐ DISCOURAGED
☐ HOPEFUL   ☐ DRAINED
☐ LOVING   ☐ SAD
☐ CONNECTED   ☐ SCARED
☐ BALANCED   ☐ ANGRY
☐ JOYFUL   ☐ ANNOYED
☐ RELAXED   ☐ ANXIOUS
☐ CREATIVE   ☐ STRESSED
☐ EXCITED   ☐ OVERWHELMED
☐ _____   ☐ _____

A POSITIVE THOUGHT TO CARRY ME TO SLEEP:

_____

_____

MORNING MEDITATION DATE __/__/__

TODAY'S FOCUS:

_____

_____

_____

_____

AN AFFIRMATION FOR TODAY:

_____

_____

_____

_____

WHAT I'M GRATEFUL FOR:

_____

_____

_____

_____

_____

_____

_____

_____

WHAT I'M EXCITED ABOUT TODAY:

_____

_____

_____

HOW I'LL MAKE SPACE FOR GRATITUDE TODAY:

_____

_____

DATE ___/___/___ # EVENING REFLECTION

GOOD THINGS THAT HAPPENED TODAY:

THINGS I DID TO MAKE A POSITIVE DIFFERENCE TODAY:

HOW I FELT TODAY:

☐ HAPPY	☐ NEUTRAL
☐ CONTENT	☐ INSECURE
☐ PROUD	☐ DISCOURAGED
☐ HOPEFUL	☐ DRAINED
☐ LOVING	☐ SAD
☐ CONNECTED	☐ SCARED
☐ BALANCED	☐ ANGRY
☐ JOYFUL	☐ ANNOYED
☐ RELAXED	☐ ANXIOUS
☐ CREATIVE	☐ STRESSED
☐ EXCITED	☐ OVERWHELMED
☐ _____	☐ _____

A POSITIVE THOUGHT TO CARRY ME TO SLEEP:

MORNING MEDITATION

DATE ___/___/___

TODAY'S FOCUS:

_____
_____
_____
_____

AN AFFIRMATION FOR TODAY:

_____
_____
_____

WHAT I'M GRATEFUL FOR:

_____
_____
_____
_____
_____
_____
_____
_____

WHAT I'M EXCITED ABOUT TODAY:

_____
_____
_____

HOW I'LL MAKE SPACE FOR GRATITUDE TODAY:

_____
_____

DATE __/__/__ # EVENING REFLECTION

GOOD THINGS THAT HAPPENED TODAY:

THINGS I DID TO MAKE A POSITIVE DIFFERENCE TODAY:

HOW I FELT TODAY:

☐ HAPPY	☐ NEUTRAL
☐ CONTENT	☐ INSECURE
☐ PROUD	☐ DISCOURAGED
☐ HOPEFUL	☐ DRAINED
☐ LOVING	☐ SAD
☐ CONNECTED	☐ SCARED
☐ BALANCED	☐ ANGRY
☐ JOYFUL	☐ ANNOYED
☐ RELAXED	☐ ANXIOUS
☐ CREATIVE	☐ STRESSED
☐ EXCITED	☐ OVERWHELMED
☐ _____	☐ _____

A POSITIVE THOUGHT TO CARRY ME TO SLEEP:

MORNING MEDITATION

DATE ___/___/___

TODAY'S FOCUS:

AN AFFIRMATION FOR TODAY:

WHAT I'M GRATEFUL FOR:

WHAT I'M EXCITED ABOUT TODAY:

HOW I'LL MAKE SPACE FOR GRATITUDE TODAY:

EVENING REFLECTION

GOOD THINGS THAT HAPPENED TODAY:

THINGS I DID TO MAKE A POSITIVE DIFFERENCE TODAY:

HOW I FELT TODAY:

☐ HAPPY	☐ NEUTRAL
☐ CONTENT	☐ INSECURE
☐ PROUD	☐ DISCOURAGED
☐ HOPEFUL	☐ DRAINED
☐ LOVING	☐ SAD
☐ CONNECTED	☐ SCARED
☐ BALANCED	☐ ANGRY
☐ JOYFUL	☐ ANNOYED
☐ RELAXED	☐ ANXIOUS
☐ CREATIVE	☐ STRESSED
☐ EXCITED	☐ OVERWHELMED
☐ _____	☐ _____

A POSITIVE THOUGHT TO CARRY ME TO SLEEP:

MORNING MEDITATION

TODAY'S FOCUS:

_____

_____

_____

_____

AN AFFIRMATION FOR TODAY:

_____

_____

_____

WHAT I'M GRATEFUL FOR:

_____

_____

_____

_____

_____

_____

_____

_____

WHAT I'M EXCITED ABOUT TODAY:

_____

_____

_____

HOW I'LL MAKE SPACE FOR GRATITUDE TODAY:

_____

_____

DATE __/__/__ # EVENING REFLECTION

GOOD THINGS THAT HAPPENED TODAY:

_____

_____

_____

_____

THINGS I DID TO MAKE A POSITIVE DIFFERENCE TODAY:

_____

_____

_____

HOW I FELT TODAY:

☐ HAPPY   ☐ NEUTRAL

☐ CONTENT   ☐ INSECURE

☐ PROUD   ☐ DISCOURAGED

☐ HOPEFUL   ☐ DRAINED

☐ LOVING   ☐ SAD

☐ CONNECTED   ☐ SCARED

☐ BALANCED   ☐ ANGRY

☐ JOYFUL   ☐ ANNOYED

☐ RELAXED   ☐ ANXIOUS

☐ CREATIVE   ☐ STRESSED

☐ EXCITED   ☐ OVERWHELMED

☐ _____   ☐ _____

A POSITIVE THOUGHT TO CARRY ME TO SLEEP:

_____

_____

_____

MORNING MEDITATION

DATE ___/___/___

TODAY'S FOCUS:

AN AFFIRMATION FOR TODAY:

WHAT I'M GRATEFUL FOR:

WHAT I'M EXCITED ABOUT TODAY:

HOW I'LL MAKE SPACE FOR GRATITUDE TODAY:

DATE ___/___/___ # EVENING REFLECTION

GOOD THINGS THAT HAPPENED TODAY:

THINGS I DID TO MAKE A POSITIVE DIFFERENCE TODAY:

HOW I FELT TODAY:

- ☐ HAPPY
- ☐ CONTENT
- ☐ PROUD
- ☐ HOPEFUL
- ☐ LOVING
- ☐ CONNECTED
- ☐ BALANCED
- ☐ JOYFUL
- ☐ RELAXED
- ☐ CREATIVE
- ☐ EXCITED
- ☐ _____

- ☐ NEUTRAL
- ☐ INSECURE
- ☐ DISCOURAGED
- ☐ DRAINED
- ☐ SAD
- ☐ SCARED
- ☐ ANGRY
- ☐ ANNOYED
- ☐ ANXIOUS
- ☐ STRESSED
- ☐ OVERWHELMED
- ☐ _____

A POSITIVE THOUGHT TO CARRY ME TO SLEEP:

MORNING MEDITATION

DATE __/__/__

TODAY'S FOCUS:

AN AFFIRMATION FOR TODAY:

WHAT I'M GRATEFUL FOR:

WHAT I'M EXCITED ABOUT TODAY:

HOW I'LL MAKE SPACE FOR GRATITUDE TODAY:

DATE ___/___/___   # EVENING REFLECTION

GOOD THINGS THAT HAPPENED TODAY:

THINGS I DID TO MAKE A POSITIVE DIFFERENCE TODAY:

HOW I FELT TODAY:

☐ HAPPY   ☐ NEUTRAL
☐ CONTENT   ☐ INSECURE
☐ PROUD   ☐ DISCOURAGED
☐ HOPEFUL   ☐ DRAINED
☐ LOVING   ☐ SAD
☐ CONNECTED   ☐ SCARED
☐ BALANCED   ☐ ANGRY
☐ JOYFUL   ☐ ANNOYED
☐ RELAXED   ☐ ANXIOUS
☐ CREATIVE   ☐ STRESSED
☐ EXCITED   ☐ OVERWHELMED
☐ _____   ☐ _____

A POSITIVE THOUGHT TO CARRY ME TO SLEEP:

MORNING MEDITATION DATE ___/___/___

TODAY'S FOCUS:
_____
_____
_____
_____

AN AFFIRMATION FOR TODAY:
_____
_____
_____
_____

WHAT I'M GRATEFUL FOR:
_____
_____
_____
_____
_____
_____
_____
_____

WHAT I'M EXCITED ABOUT TODAY:
_____
_____
_____

HOW I'LL MAKE SPACE FOR GRATITUDE TODAY:
_____
_____

EVENING REFLECTION

GOOD THINGS THAT HAPPENED TODAY:

THINGS I DID TO MAKE A POSITIVE DIFFERENCE TODAY:

HOW I FELT TODAY:

- ☐ HAPPY
- ☐ CONTENT
- ☐ PROUD
- ☐ HOPEFUL
- ☐ LOVING
- ☐ CONNECTED
- ☐ BALANCED
- ☐ JOYFUL
- ☐ RELAXED
- ☐ CREATIVE
- ☐ EXCITED
- ☐ _____

- ☐ NEUTRAL
- ☐ INSECURE
- ☐ DISCOURAGED
- ☐ DRAINED
- ☐ SAD
- ☐ SCARED
- ☐ ANGRY
- ☐ ANNOYED
- ☐ ANXIOUS
- ☐ STRESSED
- ☐ OVERWHELMED
- ☐ _____

A POSITIVE THOUGHT TO CARRY ME TO SLEEP:

MORNING MEDITATION

DATE ___/___/___

TODAY'S FOCUS:

_____
_____
_____
_____

AN AFFIRMATION FOR TODAY:

_____
_____
_____
_____

WHAT I'M GRATEFUL FOR:

_____
_____
_____
_____
_____
_____
_____
_____

WHAT I'M EXCITED ABOUT TODAY:

_____
_____
_____

HOW I'LL MAKE SPACE FOR GRATITUDE TODAY:

_____
_____

DATE __/__/__ # EVENING REFLECTION

GOOD THINGS THAT HAPPENED TODAY:

_____

_____

_____

_____

THINGS I DID TO MAKE A POSITIVE DIFFERENCE TODAY:

_____

_____

_____

HOW I FELT TODAY: NOTES:

☐ HAPPY	☐ NEUTRAL	
☐ CONTENT	☐ INSECURE	
☐ PROUD	☐ DISCOURAGED	
☐ HOPEFUL	☐ DRAINED	
☐ LOVING	☐ SAD	
☐ CONNECTED	☐ SCARED	
☐ BALANCED	☐ ANGRY	
☐ JOYFUL	☐ ANNOYED	
☐ RELAXED	☐ ANXIOUS	
☐ CREATIVE	☐ STRESSED	
☐ EXCITED	☐ OVERWHELMED	
☐ _____	☐ _____	

A POSITIVE THOUGHT TO CARRY ME TO SLEEP:

_____

_____

MORNING MEDITATION

DATE ___/___/___

TODAY'S FOCUS:

AN AFFIRMATION FOR TODAY:

WHAT I'M GRATEFUL FOR:

WHAT I'M EXCITED ABOUT TODAY:

HOW I'LL MAKE SPACE FOR GRATITUDE TODAY:

DATE __/__/__ # EVENING REFLECTION

GOOD THINGS THAT HAPPENED TODAY:

THINGS I DID TO MAKE A POSITIVE DIFFERENCE TODAY:

HOW I FELT TODAY: NOTES:

☐ HAPPY   ☐ NEUTRAL
☐ CONTENT   ☐ INSECURE
☐ PROUD   ☐ DISCOURAGED
☐ HOPEFUL   ☐ DRAINED
☐ LOVING   ☐ SAD
☐ CONNECTED   ☐ SCARED
☐ BALANCED   ☐ ANGRY
☐ JOYFUL   ☐ ANNOYED
☐ RELAXED   ☐ ANXIOUS
☐ CREATIVE   ☐ STRESSED
☐ EXCITED   ☐ OVERWHELMED
☐ _____   ☐ _____

A POSITIVE THOUGHT TO CARRY ME TO SLEEP:

MORNING MEDITATION

DATE ___/___/___

TODAY'S FOCUS:

AN AFFIRMATION FOR TODAY:

WHAT I'M GRATEFUL FOR:

WHAT I'M EXCITED ABOUT TODAY:

HOW I'LL MAKE SPACE FOR GRATITUDE TODAY:

DATE __/__/__   # EVENING REFLECTION

GOOD THINGS THAT HAPPENED TODAY:

THINGS I DID TO MAKE A POSITIVE DIFFERENCE TODAY:

HOW I FELT TODAY: NOTES:

☐ HAPPY   ☐ NEUTRAL
☐ CONTENT   ☐ INSECURE
☐ PROUD   ☐ DISCOURAGED
☐ HOPEFUL   ☐ DRAINED
☐ LOVING   ☐ SAD
☐ CONNECTED   ☐ SCARED
☐ BALANCED   ☐ ANGRY
☐ JOYFUL   ☐ ANNOYED
☐ RELAXED   ☐ ANXIOUS
☐ CREATIVE   ☐ STRESSED
☐ EXCITED   ☐ OVERWHELMED
☐ _____   ☐ _____

A POSITIVE THOUGHT TO CARRY ME TO SLEEP:

MORNING MEDITATION

DATE ___/___/___

TODAY'S FOCUS:

_____

_____

_____

_____

AN AFFIRMATION FOR TODAY:

_____

_____

_____

WHAT I'M GRATEFUL FOR:

_____

_____

_____

_____

_____

_____

_____

_____

_____

WHAT I'M EXCITED ABOUT TODAY:

_____

_____

_____

HOW I'LL MAKE SPACE FOR GRATITUDE TODAY:

_____

_____

DATE __/__/__ # EVENING REFLECTION

GOOD THINGS THAT HAPPENED TODAY:

_____

_____

_____

THINGS I DID TO MAKE A POSITIVE DIFFERENCE TODAY:

_____

_____

_____

HOW I FELT TODAY: NOTES:

- ☐ HAPPY   ☐ NEUTRAL
- ☐ CONTENT   ☐ INSECURE
- ☐ PROUD   ☐ DISCOURAGED
- ☐ HOPEFUL   ☐ DRAINED
- ☐ LOVING   ☐ SAD
- ☐ CONNECTED   ☐ SCARED
- ☐ BALANCED   ☐ ANGRY
- ☐ JOYFUL   ☐ ANNOYED
- ☐ RELAXED   ☐ ANXIOUS
- ☐ CREATIVE   ☐ STRESSED
- ☐ EXCITED   ☐ OVERWHELMED
- ☐ _____   ☐ _____

A POSITIVE THOUGHT TO CARRY ME TO SLEEP:

_____

_____

MORNING MEDITATION

DATE ___/___/___

TODAY'S FOCUS:

AN AFFIRMATION FOR TODAY:

WHAT I'M GRATEFUL FOR:

WHAT I'M EXCITED ABOUT TODAY:

HOW I'LL MAKE SPACE FOR GRATITUDE TODAY:

DATE ___/___/___ # EVENING REFLECTION

GOOD THINGS THAT HAPPENED TODAY:

THINGS I DID TO MAKE A POSITIVE DIFFERENCE TODAY:

HOW I FELT TODAY: NOTES:

☐ HAPPY   ☐ NEUTRAL

☐ CONTENT   ☐ INSECURE

☐ PROUD   ☐ DISCOURAGED

☐ HOPEFUL   ☐ DRAINED

☐ LOVING   ☐ SAD

☐ CONNECTED   ☐ SCARED

☐ BALANCED   ☐ ANGRY

☐ JOYFUL   ☐ ANNOYED

☐ RELAXED   ☐ ANXIOUS

☐ CREATIVE   ☐ STRESSED

☐ EXCITED   ☐ OVERWHELMED

☐ _____   ☐ _____

A POSITIVE THOUGHT TO CARRY ME TO SLEEP:

MORNING MEDITATION

TODAY'S FOCUS:

AN AFFIRMATION FOR TODAY:

WHAT I'M GRATEFUL FOR:

WHAT I'M EXCITED ABOUT TODAY:

HOW I'LL MAKE SPACE FOR GRATITUDE TODAY:

DATE ___/___/___   # EVENING REFLECTION

GOOD THINGS THAT HAPPENED TODAY:

THINGS I DID TO MAKE A POSITIVE DIFFERENCE TODAY:

HOW I FELT TODAY: NOTES:

- [ ] HAPPY   [ ] NEUTRAL
- [ ] CONTENT   [ ] INSECURE
- [ ] PROUD   [ ] DISCOURAGED
- [ ] HOPEFUL   [ ] DRAINED
- [ ] LOVING   [ ] SAD
- [ ] CONNECTED   [ ] SCARED
- [ ] BALANCED   [ ] ANGRY
- [ ] JOYFUL   [ ] ANNOYED
- [ ] RELAXED   [ ] ANXIOUS
- [ ] CREATIVE   [ ] STRESSED
- [ ] EXCITED   [ ] OVERWHELMED
- [ ] _____   [ ] _____

A POSITIVE THOUGHT TO CARRY ME TO SLEEP:

MORNING MEDITATION DATE __/__/__

TODAY'S FOCUS:

AN AFFIRMATION FOR TODAY:

WHAT I'M GRATEFUL FOR:

WHAT I'M EXCITED ABOUT TODAY:

HOW I'LL MAKE SPACE FOR GRATITUDE TODAY:

DATE __/__/__ # EVENING REFLECTION

GOOD THINGS THAT HAPPENED TODAY:

THINGS I DID TO MAKE A POSITIVE DIFFERENCE TODAY:

HOW I FELT TODAY: NOTES:

☐ HAPPY   ☐ NEUTRAL
☐ CONTENT   ☐ INSECURE
☐ PROUD   ☐ DISCOURAGED
☐ HOPEFUL   ☐ DRAINED
☐ LOVING   ☐ SAD
☐ CONNECTED   ☐ SCARED
☐ BALANCED   ☐ ANGRY
☐ JOYFUL   ☐ ANNOYED
☐ RELAXED   ☐ ANXIOUS
☐ CREATIVE   ☐ STRESSED
☐ EXCITED   ☐ OVERWHELMED
☐ _____   ☐ _____

A POSITIVE THOUGHT TO CARRY ME TO SLEEP:

MORNING MEDITATION

DATE ___/___/___

TODAY'S FOCUS:

AN AFFIRMATION FOR TODAY:

WHAT I'M GRATEFUL FOR:

WHAT I'M EXCITED ABOUT TODAY:

HOW I'LL MAKE SPACE FOR GRATITUDE TODAY:

DATE __/__/__ EVENING REFLECTION

GOOD THINGS THAT HAPPENED TODAY:

THINGS I DID TO MAKE A POSITIVE DIFFERENCE TODAY:

HOW I FELT TODAY: NOTES:

- [ ] HAPPY   - [ ] NEUTRAL
- [ ] CONTENT   - [ ] INSECURE
- [ ] PROUD   - [ ] DISCOURAGED
- [ ] HOPEFUL   - [ ] DRAINED
- [ ] LOVING   - [ ] SAD
- [ ] CONNECTED   - [ ] SCARED
- [ ] BALANCED   - [ ] ANGRY
- [ ] JOYFUL   - [ ] ANNOYED
- [ ] RELAXED   - [ ] ANXIOUS
- [ ] CREATIVE   - [ ] STRESSED
- [ ] EXCITED   - [ ] OVERWHELMED
- [ ] _____   - [ ] _____

A POSITIVE THOUGHT TO CARRY ME TO SLEEP:

MORNING MEDITATION

DATE __/__/__

TODAY'S FOCUS:

AN AFFIRMATION FOR TODAY:

WHAT I'M GRATEFUL FOR:

WHAT I'M EXCITED ABOUT TODAY:

HOW I'LL MAKE SPACE FOR GRATITUDE TODAY:

DATE ___/___/___ # EVENING REFLECTION

GOOD THINGS THAT HAPPENED TODAY:

THINGS I DID TO MAKE A POSITIVE DIFFERENCE TODAY:

HOW I FELT TODAY: NOTES:

- [ ] HAPPY   [ ] NEUTRAL
- [ ] CONTENT   [ ] INSECURE
- [ ] PROUD   [ ] DISCOURAGED
- [ ] HOPEFUL   [ ] DRAINED
- [ ] LOVING   [ ] SAD
- [ ] CONNECTED   [ ] SCARED
- [ ] BALANCED   [ ] ANGRY
- [ ] JOYFUL   [ ] ANNOYED
- [ ] RELAXED   [ ] ANXIOUS
- [ ] CREATIVE   [ ] STRESSED
- [ ] EXCITED   [ ] OVERWHELMED
- [ ] _____   [ ] _____

A POSITIVE THOUGHT TO CARRY ME TO SLEEP:

MORNING MEDITATION   DATE __/__/__

TODAY'S FOCUS:

_____

_____

_____

_____

AN AFFIRMATION FOR TODAY:

_____

_____

_____

WHAT I'M GRATEFUL FOR:

_____

_____

_____

_____

_____

_____

_____

_____

WHAT I'M EXCITED ABOUT TODAY:

_____

_____

_____

HOW I'LL MAKE SPACE FOR GRATITUDE TODAY:

_____

_____

DATE ___/___/___ # EVENING REFLECTION

GOOD THINGS THAT HAPPENED TODAY:

_____
_____
_____
_____

THINGS I DID TO MAKE A POSITIVE DIFFERENCE TODAY:

_____
_____
_____

HOW I FELT TODAY:

NOTES:

☐ HAPPY	☐ NEUTRAL
☐ CONTENT	☐ INSECURE
☐ PROUD	☐ DISCOURAGED
☐ HOPEFUL	☐ DRAINED
☐ LOVING	☐ SAD
☐ CONNECTED	☐ SCARED
☐ BALANCED	☐ ANGRY
☐ JOYFUL	☐ ANNOYED
☐ RELAXED	☐ ANXIOUS
☐ CREATIVE	☐ STRESSED
☐ EXCITED	☐ OVERWHELMED
☐ _____	☐ _____

A POSITIVE THOUGHT TO CARRY ME TO SLEEP:

_____
_____
_____

MORNING MEDITATION

TODAY'S FOCUS:

_____
_____
_____
_____

AN AFFIRMATION FOR TODAY:

_____
_____
_____
_____

WHAT I'M GRATEFUL FOR:

_____
_____
_____
_____
_____
_____
_____
_____

WHAT I'M EXCITED ABOUT TODAY:

_____
_____
_____
_____

HOW I'LL MAKE SPACE FOR GRATITUDE TODAY:

_____
_____
_____

DATE ___/___/___ # EVENING REFLECTION

GOOD THINGS THAT HAPPENED TODAY:

THINGS I DID TO MAKE A POSITIVE DIFFERENCE TODAY:

HOW I FELT TODAY:

☐ HAPPY	☐ NEUTRAL	**NOTES:**
☐ CONTENT	☐ INSECURE	
☐ PROUD	☐ DISCOURAGED	
☐ HOPEFUL	☐ DRAINED	
☐ LOVING	☐ SAD	
☐ CONNECTED	☐ SCARED	
☐ BALANCED	☐ ANGRY	
☐ JOYFUL	☐ ANNOYED	
☐ RELAXED	☐ ANXIOUS	
☐ CREATIVE	☐ STRESSED	
☐ EXCITED	☐ OVERWHELMED	
☐ _____	☐ _____	

A POSITIVE THOUGHT TO CARRY ME TO SLEEP:

MORNING MEDITATION

DATE ___/___/___

TODAY'S FOCUS:

_____
_____
_____
_____

AN AFFIRMATION FOR TODAY:

_____
_____
_____
_____

WHAT I'M GRATEFUL FOR:

_____
_____
_____
_____
_____
_____
_____
_____

WHAT I'M EXCITED ABOUT TODAY:

_____
_____
_____

HOW I'LL MAKE SPACE FOR GRATITUDE TODAY:

_____
_____
_____

DATE __/__/__ # EVENING REFLECTION

GOOD THINGS THAT HAPPENED TODAY:

_____

_____

_____

_____

THINGS I DID TO MAKE A POSITIVE DIFFERENCE TODAY:

_____

_____

_____

HOW I FELT TODAY:

NOTES:

☐ HAPPY ☐ NEUTRAL

☐ CONTENT ☐ INSECURE _____

☐ PROUD ☐ DISCOURAGED _____

☐ HOPEFUL ☐ DRAINED _____

☐ LOVING ☐ SAD _____

☐ CONNECTED ☐ SCARED _____

☐ BALANCED ☐ ANGRY _____

☐ JOYFUL ☐ ANNOYED _____

☐ RELAXED ☐ ANXIOUS _____

☐ CREATIVE ☐ STRESSED _____

☐ EXCITED ☐ OVERWHELMED _____

☐ _____ ☐ _____ _____

A POSITIVE THOUGHT TO CARRY ME TO SLEEP:

_____

_____

_____

MORNING MEDITATION

DATE __/__/__

TODAY'S FOCUS:

_____

_____

_____

_____

AN AFFIRMATION FOR TODAY:

_____

_____

_____

_____

WHAT I'M GRATEFUL FOR:

_____

_____

_____

_____

_____

_____

_____

_____

WHAT I'M EXCITED ABOUT TODAY:

_____

_____

_____

_____

HOW I'LL MAKE SPACE FOR GRATITUDE TODAY:

_____

_____

_____

DATE __/__/__ # EVENING REFLECTION

GOOD THINGS THAT HAPPENED TODAY:

THINGS I DID TO MAKE A POSITIVE DIFFERENCE TODAY:

HOW I FELT TODAY:

NOTES:

- [ ] HAPPY
- [ ] CONTENT
- [ ] PROUD
- [ ] HOPEFUL
- [ ] LOVING
- [ ] CONNECTED
- [ ] BALANCED
- [ ] JOYFUL
- [ ] RELAXED
- [ ] CREATIVE
- [ ] EXCITED
- [ ] _____

- [ ] NEUTRAL
- [ ] INSECURE
- [ ] DISCOURAGED
- [ ] DRAINED
- [ ] SAD
- [ ] SCARED
- [ ] ANGRY
- [ ] ANNOYED
- [ ] ANXIOUS
- [ ] STRESSED
- [ ] OVERWHELMED
- [ ] _____

A POSITIVE THOUGHT TO CARRY ME TO SLEEP:

MORNING MEDITATION

DATE ___/___/___

TODAY'S FOCUS:

_____
_____
_____
_____

AN AFFIRMATION FOR TODAY:

_____
_____
_____
_____

WHAT I'M GRATEFUL FOR:

_____
_____
_____
_____
_____
_____
_____
_____

WHAT I'M EXCITED ABOUT TODAY:

_____
_____
_____

HOW I'LL MAKE SPACE FOR GRATITUDE TODAY:

_____
_____
_____

EVENING REFLECTION

GOOD THINGS THAT HAPPENED TODAY:

THINGS I DID TO MAKE A POSITIVE DIFFERENCE TODAY:

HOW I FELT TODAY:

- [ ] HAPPY
- [ ] CONTENT
- [ ] PROUD
- [ ] HOPEFUL
- [ ] LOVING
- [ ] CONNECTED
- [ ] BALANCED
- [ ] JOYFUL
- [ ] RELAXED
- [ ] CREATIVE
- [ ] EXCITED
- [ ] _____

- [ ] NEUTRAL
- [ ] INSECURE
- [ ] DISCOURAGED
- [ ] DRAINED
- [ ] SAD
- [ ] SCARED
- [ ] ANGRY
- [ ] ANNOYED
- [ ] ANXIOUS
- [ ] STRESSED
- [ ] OVERWHELMED
- [ ] _____

NOTES:

A POSITIVE THOUGHT TO CARRY ME TO SLEEP:

MORNING MEDITATION

DATE ___/___/___

TODAY'S FOCUS:

AN AFFIRMATION FOR TODAY:

WHAT I'M GRATEFUL FOR:

WHAT I'M EXCITED ABOUT TODAY:

HOW I'LL MAKE SPACE FOR GRATITUDE TODAY:

DATE __/__/__ # EVENING REFLECTION

GOOD THINGS THAT HAPPENED TODAY:

_____

_____

_____

_____

THINGS I DID TO MAKE A POSITIVE DIFFERENCE TODAY:

_____

_____

_____

_____

HOW I FELT TODAY:

☐ HAPPY	☐ NEUTRAL		**NOTES:**
☐ CONTENT	☐ INSECURE		
☐ PROUD	☐ DISCOURAGED		_____
☐ HOPEFUL	☐ DRAINED		_____
☐ LOVING	☐ SAD		_____
☐ CONNECTED	☐ SCARED		_____
☐ BALANCED	☐ ANGRY		_____
☐ JOYFUL	☐ ANNOYED		_____
☐ RELAXED	☐ ANXIOUS		_____
☐ CREATIVE	☐ STRESSED		_____
☐ EXCITED	☐ OVERWHELMED		_____
☐ _____	☐ _____		_____

A POSITIVE THOUGHT TO CARRY ME TO SLEEP:

_____

_____

_____

MORNING MEDITATION DATE __/__/__

TODAY'S FOCUS:

_____
_____
_____
_____

AN AFFIRMATION FOR TODAY:

_____
_____
_____
_____

WHAT I'M GRATEFUL FOR:

_____
_____
_____
_____
_____
_____
_____
_____

WHAT I'M EXCITED ABOUT TODAY:

_____
_____
_____

HOW I'LL MAKE SPACE FOR GRATITUDE TODAY:

_____
_____
_____

DATE __/__/__ # EVENING REFLECTION

GOOD THINGS THAT HAPPENED TODAY:

THINGS I DID TO MAKE A POSITIVE DIFFERENCE TODAY:

HOW I FELT TODAY:

☐ HAPPY	☐ NEUTRAL
☐ CONTENT	☐ INSECURE
☐ PROUD	☐ DISCOURAGED
☐ HOPEFUL	☐ DRAINED
☐ LOVING	☐ SAD
☐ CONNECTED	☐ SCARED
☐ BALANCED	☐ ANGRY
☐ JOYFUL	☐ ANNOYED
☐ RELAXED	☐ ANXIOUS
☐ CREATIVE	☐ STRESSED
☐ EXCITED	☐ OVERWHELMED
☐ _____	☐ _____

NOTES:

A POSITIVE THOUGHT TO CARRY ME TO SLEEP:

MORNING MEDITATION DATE __/__/__

TODAY'S FOCUS:

_____

_____

_____

_____

AN AFFIRMATION FOR TODAY:

_____

_____

_____

_____

WHAT I'M GRATEFUL FOR:

_____

_____

_____

_____

_____

_____

_____

_____

WHAT I'M EXCITED ABOUT TODAY:

_____

_____

_____

_____

HOW I'LL MAKE SPACE FOR GRATITUDE TODAY:

_____

_____

_____

DATE __/__/__ # EVENING REFLECTION

GOOD THINGS THAT HAPPENED TODAY:

THINGS I DID TO MAKE A POSITIVE DIFFERENCE TODAY:

HOW I FELT TODAY:

NOTES:

- ☐ HAPPY
- ☐ CONTENT
- ☐ PROUD
- ☐ HOPEFUL
- ☐ LOVING
- ☐ CONNECTED
- ☐ BALANCED
- ☐ JOYFUL
- ☐ RELAXED
- ☐ CREATIVE
- ☐ EXCITED
- ☐ _____

- ☐ NEUTRAL
- ☐ INSECURE
- ☐ DISCOURAGED
- ☐ DRAINED
- ☐ SAD
- ☐ SCARED
- ☐ ANGRY
- ☐ ANNOYED
- ☐ ANXIOUS
- ☐ STRESSED
- ☐ OVERWHELMED
- ☐ _____

A POSITIVE THOUGHT TO CARRY ME TO SLEEP:

MORNING MEDITATION

DATE ___/___/___

TODAY'S FOCUS:

_____

_____

_____

AN AFFIRMATION FOR TODAY:

_____

_____

_____

WHAT I'M GRATEFUL FOR:

_____

_____

_____

_____

_____

_____

WHAT I'M EXCITED ABOUT TODAY:

_____

_____

_____

HOW I'LL MAKE SPACE FOR GRATITUDE TODAY:

_____

_____

EVENING REFLECTION

DATE __/__/__

GOOD THINGS THAT HAPPENED TODAY:

THINGS I DID TO MAKE A POSITIVE DIFFERENCE TODAY:

HOW I FELT TODAY:

- ☐ HAPPY
- ☐ CONTENT
- ☐ PROUD
- ☐ HOPEFUL
- ☐ LOVING
- ☐ CONNECTED
- ☐ BALANCED
- ☐ JOYFUL
- ☐ RELAXED
- ☐ CREATIVE
- ☐ EXCITED
- ☐ _____

- ☐ NEUTRAL
- ☐ INSECURE
- ☐ DISCOURAGED
- ☐ DRAINED
- ☐ SAD
- ☐ SCARED
- ☐ ANGRY
- ☐ ANNOYED
- ☐ ANXIOUS
- ☐ STRESSED
- ☐ OVERWHELMED
- ☐ _____

NOTES:

A POSITIVE THOUGHT TO CARRY ME TO SLEEP:

MORNING MEDITATION

DATE ___/___/___

TODAY'S FOCUS:

AN AFFIRMATION FOR TODAY:

WHAT I'M GRATEFUL FOR:

WHAT I'M EXCITED ABOUT TODAY:

HOW I'LL MAKE SPACE FOR GRATITUDE TODAY:

DATE __/__/__ # EVENING REFLECTION

GOOD THINGS THAT HAPPENED TODAY:

THINGS I DID TO MAKE A POSITIVE DIFFERENCE TODAY:

HOW I FELT TODAY:

☐ HAPPY   ☐ NEUTRAL
☐ CONTENT   ☐ INSECURE
☐ PROUD   ☐ DISCOURAGED
☐ HOPEFUL   ☐ DRAINED
☐ LOVING   ☐ SAD
☐ CONNECTED   ☐ SCARED
☐ BALANCED   ☐ ANGRY
☐ JOYFUL   ☐ ANNOYED
☐ RELAXED   ☐ ANXIOUS
☐ CREATIVE   ☐ STRESSED
☐ EXCITED   ☐ OVERWHELMED
☐ _____   ☐ _____

A POSITIVE THOUGHT TO CARRY ME TO SLEEP:

MORNING MEDITATION

DATE ___/___/___

TODAY'S FOCUS:

_____

_____

_____

_____

AN AFFIRMATION FOR TODAY:

_____

_____

_____

WHAT I'M GRATEFUL FOR:

_____

_____

_____

_____

_____

_____

_____

WHAT I'M EXCITED ABOUT TODAY:

_____

_____

_____

HOW I'LL MAKE SPACE FOR GRATITUDE TODAY:

_____

_____

DATE __/__/__ # EVENING REFLECTION

GOOD THINGS THAT HAPPENED TODAY:

THINGS I DID TO MAKE A POSITIVE DIFFERENCE TODAY:

HOW I FELT TODAY:

☐ HAPPY   ☐ NEUTRAL
☐ CONTENT   ☐ INSECURE
☐ PROUD   ☐ DISCOURAGED
☐ HOPEFUL   ☐ DRAINED
☐ LOVING   ☐ SAD
☐ CONNECTED   ☐ SCARED
☐ BALANCED   ☐ ANGRY
☐ JOYFUL   ☐ ANNOYED
☐ RELAXED   ☐ ANXIOUS
☐ CREATIVE   ☐ STRESSED
☐ EXCITED   ☐ OVERWHELMED
☐ _____   ☐ _____

A POSITIVE THOUGHT TO CARRY ME TO SLEEP:

MORNING MEDITATION

DATE ___/___/___

TODAY'S FOCUS:

AN AFFIRMATION FOR TODAY:

WHAT I'M GRATEFUL FOR:

WHAT I'M EXCITED ABOUT TODAY:

HOW I'LL MAKE SPACE FOR GRATITUDE TODAY:

DATE __/__/__ # EVENING REFLECTION

GOOD THINGS THAT HAPPENED TODAY:

THINGS I DID TO MAKE A POSITIVE DIFFERENCE TODAY:

HOW I FELT TODAY:

☐ HAPPY   ☐ NEUTRAL
☐ CONTENT   ☐ INSECURE
☐ PROUD   ☐ DISCOURAGED
☐ HOPEFUL   ☐ DRAINED
☐ LOVING   ☐ SAD
☐ CONNECTED   ☐ SCARED
☐ BALANCED   ☐ ANGRY
☐ JOYFUL   ☐ ANNOYED
☐ RELAXED   ☐ ANXIOUS
☐ CREATIVE   ☐ STRESSED
☐ EXCITED   ☐ OVERWHELMED
☐ _____   ☐ _____

A POSITIVE THOUGHT TO CARRY ME TO SLEEP:

MORNING MEDITATION

DATE ___/___/___

TODAY'S FOCUS:

_____

_____

_____

_____

AN AFFIRMATION FOR TODAY:

_____

_____

_____

WHAT I'M GRATEFUL FOR:

_____

_____

_____

_____

_____

_____

_____

WHAT I'M EXCITED ABOUT TODAY:

_____

_____

_____

HOW I'LL MAKE SPACE FOR GRATITUDE TODAY:

_____

_____

DATE __/__/__ # EVENING REFLECTION

GOOD THINGS THAT HAPPENED TODAY:

THINGS I DID TO MAKE A POSITIVE DIFFERENCE TODAY:

HOW I FELT TODAY:

☐ HAPPY   ☐ NEUTRAL
☐ CONTENT   ☐ INSECURE
☐ PROUD   ☐ DISCOURAGED
☐ HOPEFUL   ☐ DRAINED
☐ LOVING   ☐ SAD
☐ CONNECTED   ☐ SCARED
☐ BALANCED   ☐ ANGRY
☐ JOYFUL   ☐ ANNOYED
☐ RELAXED   ☐ ANXIOUS
☐ CREATIVE   ☐ STRESSED
☐ EXCITED   ☐ OVERWHELMED
☐ _____   ☐ _____

A POSITIVE THOUGHT TO CARRY ME TO SLEEP:

MORNING MEDITATION

DATE __/__/__

TODAY'S FOCUS:

AN AFFIRMATION FOR TODAY:

WHAT I'M GRATEFUL FOR:

WHAT I'M EXCITED ABOUT TODAY:

HOW I'LL MAKE SPACE FOR GRATITUDE TODAY:

DATE __/__/__ EVENING REFLECTION

GOOD THINGS THAT HAPPENED TODAY:

_____

_____

_____

THINGS I DID TO MAKE A POSITIVE DIFFERENCE TODAY:

_____

_____

_____

HOW I FELT TODAY:

☐ HAPPY   ☐ NEUTRAL
☐ CONTENT   ☐ INSECURE
☐ PROUD   ☐ DISCOURAGED
☐ HOPEFUL   ☐ DRAINED
☐ LOVING   ☐ SAD
☐ CONNECTED   ☐ SCARED
☐ BALANCED   ☐ ANGRY
☐ JOYFUL   ☐ ANNOYED
☐ RELAXED   ☐ ANXIOUS
☐ CREATIVE   ☐ STRESSED
☐ EXCITED   ☐ OVERWHELMED
☐ _____   ☐ _____

A POSITIVE THOUGHT TO CARRY ME TO SLEEP:

_____

_____

_____

MORNING MEDITATION

DATE ___ / ___ / ___

TODAY'S FOCUS:

_____

_____

_____

AN AFFIRMATION FOR TODAY:

_____

_____

_____

WHAT I'M GRATEFUL FOR:

_____

_____

_____

_____

_____

_____

WHAT I'M EXCITED ABOUT TODAY:

_____

_____

_____

HOW I'LL MAKE SPACE FOR GRATITUDE TODAY:

_____

_____

DATE __/__/__ EVENING REFLECTION

GOOD THINGS THAT HAPPENED TODAY:

THINGS I DID TO MAKE A POSITIVE DIFFERENCE TODAY:

HOW I FELT TODAY:

- [ ] HAPPY
- [ ] CONTENT
- [ ] PROUD
- [ ] HOPEFUL
- [ ] LOVING
- [ ] CONNECTED
- [ ] BALANCED
- [ ] JOYFUL
- [ ] RELAXED
- [ ] CREATIVE
- [ ] EXCITED
- [ ] _____

- [ ] NEUTRAL
- [ ] INSECURE
- [ ] DISCOURAGED
- [ ] DRAINED
- [ ] SAD
- [ ] SCARED
- [ ] ANGRY
- [ ] ANNOYED
- [ ] ANXIOUS
- [ ] STRESSED
- [ ] OVERWHELMED
- [ ] _____

A POSITIVE THOUGHT TO CARRY ME TO SLEEP:

MORNING MEDITATION DATE __/__/__

TODAY'S FOCUS:

_____
_____
_____
_____

AN AFFIRMATION FOR TODAY:

_____
_____
_____

WHAT I'M GRATEFUL FOR:

_____
_____
_____
_____
_____
_____
_____

WHAT I'M EXCITED ABOUT TODAY:

_____
_____
_____

HOW I'LL MAKE SPACE FOR GRATITUDE TODAY:

_____
_____

DATE ___/___/___ # EVENING REFLECTION

GOOD THINGS THAT HAPPENED TODAY:

_____

_____

_____

_____

THINGS I DID TO MAKE A POSITIVE DIFFERENCE TODAY:

_____

_____

_____

_____

HOW I FELT TODAY:

☐ HAPPY   ☐ NEUTRAL
☐ CONTENT   ☐ INSECURE
☐ PROUD   ☐ DISCOURAGED
☐ HOPEFUL   ☐ DRAINED
☐ LOVING   ☐ SAD
☐ CONNECTED   ☐ SCARED
☐ BALANCED   ☐ ANGRY
☐ JOYFUL   ☐ ANNOYED
☐ RELAXED   ☐ ANXIOUS
☐ CREATIVE   ☐ STRESSED
☐ EXCITED   ☐ OVERWHELMED
☐ _____   ☐ _____

A POSITIVE THOUGHT TO CARRY ME TO SLEEP:

_____

_____

_____

MORNING MEDITATION   DATE ___/___/___

TODAY'S FOCUS:

AN AFFIRMATION FOR TODAY:

WHAT I'M GRATEFUL FOR:

WHAT I'M EXCITED ABOUT TODAY:

HOW I'LL MAKE SPACE FOR GRATITUDE TODAY:

DATE __/__/__ # EVENING REFLECTION

GOOD THINGS THAT HAPPENED TODAY:
_____
_____
_____
_____

THINGS I DID TO MAKE A POSITIVE DIFFERENCE TODAY:
_____
_____
_____

HOW I FELT TODAY:

☐ HAPPY   ☐ NEUTRAL
☐ CONTENT   ☐ INSECURE.
☐ PROUD   ☐ DISCOURAGED
☐ HOPEFUL   ☐ DRAINED
☐ LOVING   ☐ SAD
☐ CONNECTED   ☐ SCARED
☐ BALANCED   ☐ ANGRY
☐ JOYFUL   ☐ ANNOYED
☐ RELAXED   ☐ ANXIOUS
☐ CREATIVE   ☐ STRESSED
☐ EXCITED   ☐ OVERWHELMED
☐ _____   ☐ _____

A POSITIVE THOUGHT TO CARRY ME TO SLEEP:
_____
_____
_____

MORNING MEDITATION DATE __/__/__

TODAY'S FOCUS:

AN AFFIRMATION FOR TODAY:

WHAT I'M GRATEFUL FOR:

WHAT I'M EXCITED ABOUT TODAY:

HOW I'LL MAKE SPACE FOR GRATITUDE TODAY:

EVENING REFLECTION

GOOD THINGS THAT HAPPENED TODAY:

THINGS I DID TO MAKE A POSITIVE DIFFERENCE TODAY:

HOW I FELT TODAY:

- ☐ HAPPY
- ☐ CONTENT
- ☐ PROUD
- ☐ HOPEFUL
- ☐ LOVING
- ☐ CONNECTED
- ☐ BALANCED
- ☐ JOYFUL
- ☐ RELAXED
- ☐ CREATIVE
- ☐ EXCITED
- ☐ _____

- ☐ NEUTRAL
- ☐ INSECURE
- ☐ DISCOURAGED
- ☐ DRAINED
- ☐ SAD
- ☐ SCARED
- ☐ ANGRY
- ☐ ANNOYED
- ☐ ANXIOUS
- ☐ STRESSED
- ☐ OVERWHELMED
- ☐ _____

A POSITIVE THOUGHT TO CARRY ME TO SLEEP:

MORNING MEDITATION

DATE ___/___/___

TODAY'S FOCUS:

_____

_____

_____

AN AFFIRMATION FOR TODAY:

_____

_____

_____

WHAT I'M GRATEFUL FOR:

_____

_____

_____

_____

_____

_____

WHAT I'M EXCITED ABOUT TODAY:

_____

_____

_____

HOW I'LL MAKE SPACE FOR GRATITUDE TODAY:

_____

_____

_____

DATE ___/___/___   EVENING REFLECTION

GOOD THINGS THAT HAPPENED TODAY:

THINGS I DID TO MAKE A POSITIVE DIFFERENCE TODAY:

HOW I FELT TODAY:

NOTES:

- [ ] HAPPY
- [ ] CONTENT
- [ ] PROUD
- [ ] HOPEFUL
- [ ] LOVING
- [ ] CONNECTED
- [ ] BALANCED
- [ ] JOYFUL
- [ ] RELAXED
- [ ] CREATIVE
- [ ] EXCITED
- [ ] _____

- [ ] NEUTRAL
- [ ] INSECURE
- [ ] DISCOURAGED
- [ ] DRAINED
- [ ] SAD
- [ ] SCARED
- [ ] ANGRY
- [ ] ANNOYED
- [ ] ANXIOUS
- [ ] STRESSED
- [ ] OVERWHELMED
- [ ] _____

A POSITIVE THOUGHT TO CARRY ME TO SLEEP:

MORNING MEDITATION

DATE ___/___/___

TODAY'S FOCUS:

_____

_____

_____

_____

AN AFFIRMATION FOR TODAY:

_____

_____

_____

WHAT I'M GRATEFUL FOR:

_____

_____

_____

_____

_____

_____

_____

WHAT I'M EXCITED ABOUT TODAY:

_____

_____

_____

HOW I'LL MAKE SPACE FOR GRATITUDE TODAY:

_____

_____

EVENING REFLECTION

GOOD THINGS THAT HAPPENED TODAY:

THINGS I DID TO MAKE A POSITIVE DIFFERENCE TODAY:

HOW I FELT TODAY:

- ☐ HAPPY
- ☐ CONTENT
- ☐ PROUD
- ☐ HOPEFUL
- ☐ LOVING
- ☐ CONNECTED
- ☐ BALANCED
- ☐ JOYFUL
- ☐ RELAXED
- ☐ CREATIVE
- ☐ EXCITED
- ☐ _____

- ☐ NEUTRAL
- ☐ INSECURE
- ☐ DISCOURAGED
- ☐ DRAINED
- ☐ SAD
- ☐ SCARED
- ☐ ANGRY
- ☐ ANNOYED
- ☐ ANXIOUS
- ☐ STRESSED
- ☐ OVERWHELMED
- ☐ _____

NOTES:

A POSITIVE THOUGHT TO CARRY ME TO SLEEP:

MORNING MEDITATION DATE __/__/__

TODAY'S FOCUS:

_____

_____

_____

_____

AN AFFIRMATION FOR TODAY:

_____

_____

_____

_____

WHAT I'M GRATEFUL FOR:

_____

_____

_____

_____

_____

_____

_____

_____

WHAT I'M EXCITED ABOUT TODAY:

_____

_____

_____

_____

HOW I'LL MAKE SPACE FOR GRATITUDE TODAY:

_____

_____

_____

DATE ___/___/___ # EVENING REFLECTION

GOOD THINGS THAT HAPPENED TODAY:

THINGS I DID TO MAKE A POSITIVE DIFFERENCE TODAY:

HOW I FELT TODAY:

NOTES:

- [ ] HAPPY
- [ ] CONTENT
- [ ] PROUD
- [ ] HOPEFUL
- [ ] LOVING
- [ ] CONNECTED
- [ ] BALANCED
- [ ] JOYFUL
- [ ] RELAXED
- [ ] CREATIVE
- [ ] EXCITED
- [ ] _____

- [ ] NEUTRAL
- [ ] INSECURE
- [ ] DISCOURAGED
- [ ] DRAINED
- [ ] SAD
- [ ] SCARED
- [ ] ANGRY
- [ ] ANNOYED
- [ ] ANXIOUS
- [ ] STRESSED
- [ ] OVERWHELMED
- [ ] _____

A POSITIVE THOUGHT TO CARRY ME TO SLEEP:

MORNING MEDITATION

DATE ___/___/___

TODAY'S FOCUS:

_____

_____

_____

_____

AN AFFIRMATION FOR TODAY:

_____

_____

_____

_____

WHAT I'M GRATEFUL FOR:

_____

_____

_____

_____

_____

_____

_____

_____

WHAT I'M EXCITED ABOUT TODAY:

_____

_____

_____

_____

HOW I'LL MAKE SPACE FOR GRATITUDE TODAY:

_____

_____

_____

DATE __/__/__ # EVENING REFLECTION

GOOD THINGS THAT HAPPENED TODAY:

_____
_____
_____
_____

THINGS I DID TO MAKE A POSITIVE DIFFERENCE TODAY:

_____
_____
_____
_____

HOW I FELT TODAY:

NOTES:

☐ HAPPY   ☐ NEUTRAL
☐ CONTENT   ☐ INSECURE   _____
☐ PROUD   ☐ DISCOURAGED   _____
☐ HOPEFUL   ☐ DRAINED   _____
☐ LOVING   ☐ SAD   _____
☐ CONNECTED   ☐ SCARED   _____
☐ BALANCED   ☐ ANGRY   _____
☐ JOYFUL   ☐ ANNOYED   _____
☐ RELAXED   ☐ ANXIOUS   _____
☐ CREATIVE   ☐ STRESSED   _____
☐ EXCITED   ☐ OVERWHELMED   _____
☐ _____   ☐ _____   _____

A POSITIVE THOUGHT TO CARRY ME TO SLEEP:

_____
_____

MORNING MEDITATION

DATE ___/___/___

TODAY'S FOCUS:

AN AFFIRMATION FOR TODAY:

WHAT I'M GRATEFUL FOR:

WHAT I'M EXCITED ABOUT TODAY:

HOW I'LL MAKE SPACE FOR GRATITUDE TODAY:

DATE ___/___/___ # EVENING REFLECTION

GOOD THINGS THAT HAPPENED TODAY:

_____

_____

_____

THINGS I DID TO MAKE A POSITIVE DIFFERENCE TODAY:

_____

_____

_____

HOW I FELT TODAY:

NOTES:

- ☐ HAPPY
- ☐ CONTENT
- ☐ PROUD
- ☐ HOPEFUL
- ☐ LOVING
- ☐ CONNECTED
- ☐ BALANCED
- ☐ JOYFUL
- ☐ RELAXED
- ☐ CREATIVE
- ☐ EXCITED
- ☐ _____

- ☐ NEUTRAL
- ☐ INSECURE
- ☐ DISCOURAGED
- ☐ DRAINED
- ☐ SAD
- ☐ SCARED
- ☐ ANGRY
- ☐ ANNOYED
- ☐ ANXIOUS
- ☐ STRESSED
- ☐ OVERWHELMED
- ☐ _____

A POSITIVE THOUGHT TO CARRY ME TO SLEEP:

_____

_____

MORNING MEDITATION DATE __/__/__

TODAY'S FOCUS:

AN AFFIRMATION FOR TODAY:

WHAT I'M GRATEFUL FOR:

WHAT I'M EXCITED ABOUT TODAY:

HOW I'LL MAKE SPACE FOR GRATITUDE TODAY:

DATE __/__/__ # EVENING REFLECTION

GOOD THINGS THAT HAPPENED TODAY:

_____

_____

_____

_____

THINGS I DID TO MAKE A POSITIVE DIFFERENCE TODAY:

_____

_____

_____

HOW I FELT TODAY:

NOTES:

- ☐ HAPPY
- ☐ CONTENT
- ☐ PROUD
- ☐ HOPEFUL
- ☐ LOVING
- ☐ CONNECTED
- ☐ BALANCED
- ☐ JOYFUL
- ☐ RELAXED
- ☐ CREATIVE
- ☐ EXCITED
- ☐ _____

- ☐ NEUTRAL
- ☐ INSECURE
- ☐ DISCOURAGED
- ☐ DRAINED
- ☐ SAD
- ☐ SCARED
- ☐ ANGRY
- ☐ ANNOYED
- ☐ ANXIOUS
- ☐ STRESSED
- ☐ OVERWHELMED
- ☐ _____

A POSITIVE THOUGHT TO CARRY ME TO SLEEP:

_____

_____

_____

MORNING MEDITATION

TODAY'S FOCUS:

_____

_____

_____

_____

AN AFFIRMATION FOR TODAY:

_____

_____

_____

WHAT I'M GRATEFUL FOR:

_____

_____

_____

_____

_____

_____

_____

_____

WHAT I'M EXCITED ABOUT TODAY:

_____

_____

_____

HOW I'LL MAKE SPACE FOR GRATITUDE TODAY:

_____

_____

_____

DATE ___/___/___ # EVENING REFLECTION

GOOD THINGS THAT HAPPENED TODAY:

_____

_____

_____

THINGS I DID TO MAKE A POSITIVE DIFFERENCE TODAY:

_____

_____

_____

HOW I FELT TODAY:

☐ HAPPY	☐ NEUTRAL
☐ CONTENT	☐ INSECURE
☐ PROUD	☐ DISCOURAGED
☐ HOPEFUL	☐ DRAINED
☐ LOVING	☐ SAD
☐ CONNECTED	☐ SCARED
☐ BALANCED	☐ ANGRY
☐ JOYFUL	☐ ANNOYED
☐ RELAXED	☐ ANXIOUS
☐ CREATIVE	☐ STRESSED
☐ EXCITED	☐ OVERWHELMED
☐ _____	☐ _____

NOTES:

_____

_____

_____

_____

_____

_____

_____

_____

_____

A POSITIVE THOUGHT TO CARRY ME TO SLEEP:

_____

_____

MORNING MEDITATION

DATE ___/___/___

TODAY'S FOCUS:

_____

_____

_____

_____

AN AFFIRMATION FOR TODAY:

_____

_____

_____

_____

WHAT I'M GRATEFUL FOR:

_____

_____

_____

_____

_____

_____

_____

_____

_____

WHAT I'M EXCITED ABOUT TODAY:

_____

_____

_____

_____

HOW I'LL MAKE SPACE FOR GRATITUDE TODAY:

_____

_____

_____

DATE __/__/__ # EVENING REFLECTION

GOOD THINGS THAT HAPPENED TODAY:

_____

_____

_____

_____

THINGS I DID TO MAKE A POSITIVE DIFFERENCE TODAY:

_____

_____

_____

HOW I FELT TODAY:

☐ HAPPY	☐ NEUTRAL	NOTES:
☐ CONTENT	☐ INSECURE	_____
☐ PROUD	☐ DISCOURAGED	_____
☐ HOPEFUL	☐ DRAINED	_____
☐ LOVING	☐ SAD	_____
☐ CONNECTED	☐ SCARED	_____
☐ BALANCED	☐ ANGRY	_____
☐ JOYFUL	☐ ANNOYED	_____
☐ RELAXED	☐ ANXIOUS	_____
☐ CREATIVE	☐ STRESSED	_____
☐ EXCITED	☐ OVERWHELMED	_____
☐ _____	☐ _____	_____

A POSITIVE THOUGHT TO CARRY ME TO SLEEP:

_____

_____

_____

MORNING MEDITATION

DATE __/__/__

TODAY'S FOCUS:

AN AFFIRMATION FOR TODAY:

WHAT I'M GRATEFUL FOR:

WHAT I'M EXCITED ABOUT TODAY:

HOW I'LL MAKE SPACE FOR GRATITUDE TODAY:

DATE __/__/__ # EVENING REFLECTION

GOOD THINGS THAT HAPPENED TODAY:

_____

_____

_____

_____

THINGS I DID TO MAKE A POSITIVE DIFFERENCE TODAY:

_____

_____

_____

HOW I FELT TODAY:

NOTES:

- ☐ HAPPY
- ☐ CONTENT
- ☐ PROUD
- ☐ HOPEFUL
- ☐ LOVING
- ☐ CONNECTED
- ☐ BALANCED
- ☐ JOYFUL
- ☐ RELAXED
- ☐ CREATIVE
- ☐ EXCITED
- ☐ _____

- ☐ NEUTRAL
- ☐ INSECURE
- ☐ DISCOURAGED
- ☐ DRAINED
- ☐ SAD
- ☐ SCARED
- ☐ ANGRY
- ☐ ANNOYED
- ☐ ANXIOUS
- ☐ STRESSED
- ☐ OVERWHELMED
- ☐ _____

A POSITIVE THOUGHT TO CARRY ME TO SLEEP:

_____

_____

_____

INSIGHTS

A Mandala Journal

MANDALA
PUBLISHING

www.mandalaearth.com